THE PENGUIN POETS

D58

ROBERT HERRICK

ROBERT HERRICK

POEMS FROM *Hesperides* AND
Noble Numbers

SELECTED AND INTRODUCED BY
JOHN HAYWARD

PENGUIN BOOKS

Penguin Books Ltd, Harmondsworth, Middlesex
U.S.A.: Penguin Books Inc., 3300 Clipper Mill Road, Baltimore 11, Md
AUSTRALIA: Penguin Books Pty Ltd, 762 Whitehorse Road,
Mitcham, Victoria

—

First published 1961

—

Copyright © John Hayward, 1961

—

Made and printed in Great Britain
by Richard Clay & Company Ltd,
Bungay, Suffolk

CONTENTS

INTRODUCTION

I f the modern newspaper (and its present style and idiom) had existed 300 years ago, it would have carried in the autumn of the year 1674 an obituary notice which might have read as follows:

The Reverend Robert Herrick, vicar of Dean Prior near Ashburton, Devon, from 1629 to 1647 and again from the Restoration until his death, died yesterday at his home in his eighty-fourth year. He will be remembered by an older generation as the author of a single volume of lyric poems and epigrams, 'humane and divine', which on its publication in 1648, when he was nearly sixty, received less than its due, the taste of the age having by then shown its preference for the poetry of the school of Donne to that of Jonson, Mr Herrick's acknowledged master.

Robert Herrick, who came from an old Leicestershire family, was born in London, the fourth son of Nicholas Herrick, goldsmith, by his marriage to Julian Stone, a mercer's daughter, and was baptized on 21 August 1591 at St Vedast's, Foster Lane. Fourteen months later his father was killed by a fall from an upper window of his house in Cheapside in circumstances which, though raising a suspicion of *felo de se*, were not deemed by the ecclesiastical arbitrator to justify the forfeiture of his estate. Robert Herrick thus became entitled to his portion of it, amounting to some £800, and was placed under the guardianship of his uncle William, later Sir William Herrick M.P., the goldsmith and merchant-banker.

Nothing is recorded of Robert Herrick's youth and schooling before his seventeenth year when, on 25 September 1607, he was bound apprentice for ten years to his uncle. He did not, however, complete his apprenticeship, for in 1613 he proceeded, with Sir William's blessing, to St John's College, Cambridge. There, like other undergraduates enjoying for the first time a too modest independence, he ran into difficulties and was obliged to petition his guardian for advances on his capital to enable him to pursue his studies with a quiet mind. In 1616 he transferred to Trinity Hall, where he could live more cheaply, and in due course took his Bachelor's and Master's degrees. He was ordained (in the diocese of Peterborough) in 1623.

The records again reveal nothing for the next six years other than his participation (as a chaplain to the then Duke of Buckingham) in the abortive expedition in 1627 to the Isle of Rhé. Something, nevertheless, may be inferred from the occasional verses he was writing during these years. He was, it would seem, on familiar terms with the poets associated with Ben Jonson and was himself esteemed as a poet by those amongst whom copies of his verses were then circulating in manuscript. By 1625, indeed, he was held to be the equal of Jonson and Drayton – an estimate that was not, however, to be confirmed by a printed book until nearly a quarter of a century later. A few poems meanwhile found their way into print in various collections: an epitaph (in St Margaret's, Westminster) transcribed by Stow in his *Survey of London* (1633); part of his once much admired 'Oberon's Feast' in *A Description of the King and Queene of Fayries* (1635); 'The Apparition of his Mistresse' with two others (all anonymously) in Shakespeare's *Poems* (1640); and two in Carew's *Poems* (1640). Why he refrained so long from publishing a collection of his own verses is, indeed, a puzzling question. He appears to have considered such a publication in 1640, for an entry in the Stationers' Register records '*The Several Poems* written by Robert Herrick', but a further eight years were to pass before Williams & Eglesfield offered for sale *Hesperides or, The Works both Humane & Divine of Robert Herrick Esq*. The Dedication to the Prince of Wales was an earnest of his fervent royalist sympathies.

On 2 October 1629, shortly after the death of his mother, he was admitted to the living of Dean Prior. In contrast to his life in London, life in a remote country parish was to prove at times lonely and irksome, though less so, perhaps, than his recurrent complaints in verse might suggest, for his 'jocund' temperament predisposed him to sing the pleasures of rustication, the charms of the pastoral scene, and the customs of the countryside. According to Mr Anthony Wood, 'he became much beloved by the Gentry in those parts for his florid and witty discourse'. From his own verses he can be pictured leading an agreeable if somewhat placid existence, surrounded by his pets (including, it is said, a domesticated pig) and cared for devotedly by his housekeeper, Miss Baldwin. In 1640 he appears secretly to have absented himself and to have spent some time in Westminster, where, according to report, he was a party to an illicit union. Seven years later he paid the inevitable penalty of his allegiance to the King and was ejected from his living. During the sad interim he lived in Westminster as a common citizen (dressing himself accordingly) and was dependent upon the charity of his family and his friends of earlier days. Having prepared his poems for the printer, he retired into obscurity and did not emerge from it until after the return of the King and then only briefly, to petition for his own restoration. His living was restored to him in the summer of 1662 and he returned to Dean Prior, where he passed the twelve years remaining to him. He was unmarried.

Mr Herrick wrote little if anything during the past twenty-five years and had published nothing since 1648, apart from some memorial verses for the late Lord Hastings in *Lachrymae Musarum* of the following year. Though an old-fashioned poet, now forgotten by the younger generation, Mr Herrick wrote several lyrics (notably 'To the Virgins') which have continued to appear in anthologies; and there are grounds for believing that a later age, rediscovering his verses, will fulfil the hope expressed in his epigraph to *Hesperides: Effugiunt avidos Carmina nostra Rogos.*

The funeral will take place at Dean Prior on 15 October.

*　　*　　*

So little is known about Herrick that it is tempting to read between the lines of his poems in the hope of discovering more. There are, to be sure, references in them which add a few trifling facts to his uneventful biography; and there are inferences to be drawn from them at a venture which reveal aspects of his poetic *persona*. But, though they may throw some light on an otherwise obscure country clergyman, they throw none on the nature of his poetry. And it is the poetry that matters, not the man who made it. Herrick, no doubt, is a promising subject for the kind of post-mortem analysis that seeks to explain a man's psychological constitution by his life and works. There is a morbid case-history to be compiled from such data as his father's mysterious death and his apparent neglect of his mother; his Lilliputian fantasies about fairyland; the paradox that, though he never married and affirmed that 'his life was chaste', he fed his sensibility on erotic images, and perhaps more significantly, on their ugly obverse – physical deformity and neglect, the repellent aspects of uncleanliness and intemperance, which were so patently obvious in his day as scarcely to need advertising in verse. (One thinks of that other Church of England clergyman, Jonathan Swift, whose mother coincidentally was a Leicestershire Herrick, who also expressed in verse an almost pathological disgust for certain aspects of the human body and its functions.) But psychology can no more isolate the poetic quintessence of, say, his plea 'To the Virgins, to make much of Time' or account for the poignancy of his appeal 'To Daffadils' than pomology could have explained the magic of the apples in the Garden of Hesperides.

The poems in his *Hesperides* are of four kinds: amatory,

pastoral, occasional, epigrammatic. More exactly defined, they are the short love lyrics addressed to his 'supposed' mistresses – Anthea, Dianeme, Electra, Julia, and the rest; the poems, including those about fairies, which treat more or less in the classic pastoral convention of the customs and traditions of country life; verses written for an occasion – a marriage, a death, an event of private or public interest – and offered to the person or persons involved; and the curt epigram, rarely more than two or four lines long, that attempts to characterize the whole of its victim by a part (usually an unpleasant one). Their character is succinctly summarized in 'The Argument of his Book', which is printed here before the first page of text. On the face of it the collection appears to have been put together capriciously, regardless of design or order; but it is difficult to believe that Herrick, who certainly took pains to give a correct text of his poems (to the extent of making stop-press corrections and supplying a list of petty errata), did not bother about their disposition. The apparent lack of arrangement was probably intentional, a way of avoiding possible monotony by diverting the reader with variety and – to use his own phrase – 'delight in disorder'.

Apart from those occasional pieces which can be dated from external evidence, the poems in *Hesperides* cannot be assigned to any year or even decade. The suggestion that they were printed in chronological order of composition only fixes the terminal dates, namely around 1610, when Herrick was nineteen, and 1647 (the date on the separate title to 'Noble Numbers'). Which poems were written before, and which after he settled at Dean Prior, must remain an open question. More likely than not he wrote most of his 'humane' poems before, as he certainly wrote most of his 'divine' poems after, he left London. Why Herrick delayed their publication until so late in life is a mystery. The 'humane' poems alone would have made a substantial volume, and most of them would have been ready for publication around 1630 before they had become outmoded. As it was, *Hesperides* must have struck its first readers as a curiously old-fashioned collection recalling the poetry of the first quarter of the century. Three hundred years later the reaction of readers in 1948 to the first book of an elderly 'Georgian' poet, uninfluenced by Pound and Eliot, would have been similar; they would have neglected him (as Herrick was neglected by the younger generation in favour of Donne and Cleveland and, in due course, Dryden, who was already Poet Laureate when Herrick died, forgotten and unsung, years later) – the equivalent of a contemporary of Rupert Brooke's, dying in 1972 as remote from London as a Devonshire vicarage was in the seventeenth century. Even so, when full allowance is made for changes in the climate of poetic thought and sensibility, and for corresponding revolutions in taste, it is still difficult to believe that Herrick was utterly forgotten until the beginning of the nineteenth century. The Romantic Revival 'revived' him, and in 1810 a selection of some 300 of the more than 1400 poems in *Hesperides* was published. In 1823 Thomas Maitland edited his *Complete Poems* in two volumes, and from the 1860s onwards later editors have assured them the immortality that Herrick conventionally claimed as their due. The definitive edition, in the Oxford English Texts, was prepared by Professor L. C. Martin and published by the Clarendon Press in 1956.

Herrick is not one of the very few poets whose innovations have extended the range and depth of poetic apprehension. His lack of originality is obvious in his dependence upon his chosen classical models. His verse is full of echoes and even direct imitations of Horace, Tibullus, Catullus, Ovid, and Martial; and he borrows also from the Elizabethan song-writers. Although he wanted imagination, the supreme poetic power that transforms or transmutes the elements of sensible experience, he had an extremely lively and inventive fancy and with it not only a marvellously delicate ear but also the requisite technical mastery for arranging words harmoniously in metrical patterns. His poetry, though simple and sensuous, is never passionate. If his limitations are self-evident, he is wholly at ease within them and expresses his thoughts, which are never profound, and his emotions, which are never complex, with purity, tenderness, grace, and precision. He was, perhaps, too much at ease, too fluent a composer, too ready to make a song of a trivial or whimsical reflection of sentiment, or merely to turn a commonplace into gnomic verse. In short, he wrote too much — certainly more than the most sympathetic reader can ingest without feeling surfeited. It follows, since to have too much of a good thing is to risk losing a sense of its value, that Herrick's poems are best enjoyed and valued in selection. The following selection has been designed to this end.

JOHN HAYWARD

NOTE ON THE TEXT

The text of Herrick's poems presents no problems or difficulties. He himself prepared them for publication and saw them through the press. The text of the present selection from *Hesperides* is therefore reprinted from the first edition which was published in London in 1648. The copy used for this purpose was lent by Bernard Quaritch Ltd, whose generosity is gratefully acknowledged. Only the following alterations from the copy text have been made: the original errata listed in the first edition, together with a few other misprints and space-saving contractions made by the original compositor, have been silently corrected; the archaic form of the comparative 'then' has been modernized; and lower-case 's' has been substituted for the old elongated ſ. The very few other minor corrections are enclosed by square brackets.

J. H.

FROM

Hesperides

The Argument of his Book

I sing of *Brooks*, of *Blossomes*, *Birds*, and *Bowers:*
Of *April*, *May*, of *June*, and *July*-Flowers.
I sing of *May-poles*, *Hock-carts*, *Wassails*, *Wakes*,
Of *Bride-grooms*, *Brides*, and of their *Bridall-cakes*.
I write of *Youth*, of *Love*, and have Accesse
By these, to sing of cleanly-*Wantonnesse*.
I sing of *Dewes*, of *Raines*, and piece by piece
Of *Balme*, of *Oyle*, of *Spice*, and *Amber-Greece*.
I sing of *Times trans-shifting*; and I write
How *Roses* first came *Red*, and *Lilies White*.
I write of *Groves*, of *Twilights*, and I sing
The Court of *Mab*, and of the *Fairie-King*.
I write of *Hell*; I sing (and ever shall)
Of *Heaven*, and hope to have it after all.

To his Booke

While thou didst keep thy *Candor* undefil'd,
Deerely I lov'd thee; as my first-borne child:
But when I saw thee wantonly to roame
From house to house, and never stay at home;
I brake my bonds of Love, and bad thee goe,
Regardlesse whether well thou sped'st, or no.
On with thy fortunes then, what e're they be;
If good I'le smile, if bad I'le sigh for Thee.

Upon Julias *Recovery*

Droop, droop no more, or hang the head
Ye *Roses* almost withered;
Now strength, and newer Purple get,
Each here declining *Violet*.
O *Primroses*! let this day be
A Resurrection unto ye;
And to all flowers ally'd in blood,
Or sworn to that sweet Sister-hood:
For Health on *Julia's* cheek hath shed
Clarret, and Creame commingled.
And those her lips doe now appeare
As beames of *Corrall*, but more cleare.

To Silvia *to wed*

Let us (though late) at last (my *Silvia*) wed;
And loving lie in one devoted bed.
Thy Watch may stand, my minutes fly poste haste;
No sound calls back the yeere that once is past.
Then sweetest *Silvia*, let's no longer stay;
True love, we know, precipitates delay.
Away with doubts, all scruples hence remove;
No man at one time, can be wise, and love.

The Parliament of Roses to Julia

I dreamt the Roses one time went
To meet and sit in Parliament:
The place for these, and for the rest
Of flowers, was thy spotlesse breast:
Over the which a State* was drawne
Of Tiffanie, or Cob-web Lawne;
Then in that *Parly*, all those powers
Voted the Rose; the Queen of flowers.
But so, as that her self should be
The maide of Honour unto thee.

To Perilla

Ah my *Perilla*! do'st thou grieve to see
Me, day by day, to steale away from thee?
Age cals me hence, and my gray haires bid come,
And haste away to mine eternal home;

* State = Canopy.

'Twill not be long (*Perilla*) after this,
That I must give thee the *supremest* kisse:
Dead when I am, first cast in salt, and bring
Part of the creame from that *Religious Spring*;
With which (*Perilla*) wash my hands and feet;
That done, then wind me in that very sheet
Which wrapt thy smooth limbs (when thou didst
    implore
The Gods protection, but the night before)
Follow me weeping to my Turfe, and there
Let fall a *Primrose*, and with it a teare:
Then lastly, let some weekly-strewings be
Devoted to the memory of me:
Then shall my *Ghost* not walk about, but keep
Still in the coole, and silent shades of sleep.

A Song to the Maskers

Come down, and dance ye in the toyle
    Of pleasures, to a Heate;
But if to moisture, Let the oyle
    Of Roses be your sweat.

Not only to your selves assume
    These sweets, but let them fly;
From this, to that, and so Perfume
    E'ne all the standers by.

As Goddesse *Isis* (when she went,
    Or glided through the street)
Made all that touch't her with her scent,
    And whom she touch't, turne sweet.

To his Mistresses

Helpe me! helpe me! now I call
To my pretty *Witchcrafts* all:
Old I am, and cannot do
That, I was accustom'd to.
Bring your *Magicks*, *Spels*, *and Charmes*,
To enflesh my thighs, and armes:
Is there no way to beget
In my limbs their former heat?
Æson had (as *Poets* faine)
Baths that made him young againe:
Find that *Medicine* (if you can)
For your drie-decrepid man:
Who would faine his strength renew,
Were it but to pleasure you.

No Loathsomenesse in love

What I fancy, I approve,
No Dislike there is in love:
Be my Mistresse short or tall,
And distorted there-withall:
Be she likewise one of those,
That an *Acre* hath of Nose:
Be her forehead, and her eyes
Full of incongruities:
Be her cheeks so shallow too,
As to shew her *Tongue* wag through:

Be her lips ill hung, or set,
And her grinders black as jet;
Ha's she thinne haire, hath she none,
She's to me a *Paragon*.

Soft Musick

The mellow touch of musick most doth wound
The soule, when it doth rather sigh, than sound.

His Answer to a Question

Some would know
Why I so
Long still doe tarry,
And ask why
Here that I
Live, and not marry?
Thus I those
Doe oppose;
What man would be here,
Slave to Thrall,
If at all
He could live free here?

Upon Julia's *Fall*

Julia was carelesse, and withall,
She rather took, than got a fall:
The wanton *Ambler* chanc'd to see
Part of her leggs sinceritie:
And ravish'd thus, It came to passe,
The Nagge (like to the *Prophets Asse*)
Began to speak, and would have been
A telling what rare sights h'ad seen:
And had told all; but did refraine,
Because his Tongue was ty'd againe.

Presence and Absence

When what is lov'd, is Present, love doth spring;
But being absent, Love lies languishing.

The Pomander Bracelet

To me my *Julia* lately sent
A Bracelet richly Redolent:
The Beads I kist, but most lov'd her
That did perfume the Pomander.

The shooe tying

Anthea bade me tye her shooe;
I did; and kist the Instep too:
And would have kist unto her knee,
Had not her Blush rebuked me.

How the Wall-flower came first, and why so called

Why this Flower is now call'd so,
List' sweet maids, and you shal know.
Understand, this First-ling was
Once a brisk and bonny Lasse,
Kept as close as *Danae* was:
Who a sprightly *Springall* lov'd,
And to have it fully prov'd,
Up she got upon a wall,
Tempting down to slide withall:
But the silken twist unty'd,
So she fell, and bruis'd, she dy'd.
Love, in pitty of the deed,
And her loving-lucklesse speed,
Turn'd her to this Plant, we call
Now, *The Flower of the Wall*.

To his Mistresse objecting to him neither Toying or Talking

You say I love not, 'cause I doe not play
Still with your curles, and kisse the time away.
You blame me too, because I cann't devise
Some sport, to please those Babies in your eyes:
By *Loves Religion*, I must here confesse it,
The most I love, when I the least expresse it.

Small griefs find tongues: Full Casques are ever found
To give (if any, yet) but little sound.
Deep waters noyse-lesse are; And this we know,
That chiding streams betray small depth below.
So when Love speechlesse is, she doth expresse
A depth in love, and that depth, bottomlesse.
Now since my love is tongue-lesse, know me such,
Who speak but little, 'cause I love so much.

On himselfe

Young I was, but now am old,
But I am not yet grown cold;
I can play, and I can twine
'Bout a Virgin like a Vine:
In her lap too I can lye
Melting, and in fancie die:
And return to life, if she
Claps my cheek, or kisseth me;
Thus, and thus it now appears
That our love out-lasts our yeeres.

The Parcæ, or, Three dainty Destinies

The Armilet

Three lovely Sisters working were
  (As they were closely set)
Of soft and dainty Maiden-haire,
  A curious *Armelet.*

I smiling, ask'd them what they did?
   (Faire *Destinies* all three)
Who told me, they had drawn a thred
   Of Life, and 'twas for me.
They shew'd me then, how fine 'twas spun;
   And I reply'd thereto,
I care not now how soone 'tis done,
   Or cut, if cut by you.

Cherry-pit

Julia and I did lately sit
Playing for sport, at Cherry-pit:
She threw; I cast; and having thrown,
I got the Pit, and she the Stone.

Discontents in Devon

More discontents I never had
   Since I was born, than here;
Where I have been, and still am sad,
   In this dull *Devon-shire:*
Yet justly too I must confesse;
   I ne'r invented such
Ennobled numbers for the Presse,
   Than where I loath'd so much.

Cherrie-ripe

Cherrie-Ripe, Ripe, Ripe, I cry,
Full and faire ones; come and buy:
If so be, you ask me where
They doe grow? I answer, There,
Where my *Julia's* lips doe smile;
There's the Land, or Cherry-Ile:
Whose Plantations fully show
All the yeere, where Cherries grow.

The Vision to Electra

I dream'd we both were in a bed
Of Roses, almost smothered:
The warmth and sweetnes had me there
Made lovingly familiar:
But that I heard thy sweet breath say,
Faults done by night, will blush by day:
I kist thee (panting,) and I call
Night to the Record! that was all.
But ah! if empty dreames so please,
Love give me more such nights as these.

Dreames

Here we are all, by day; By night w'are hurl'd
By dreames, each one, into a sev'rall world.

His request to Julia

Julia, if I chance to die
Ere I print my Poetry;
I most humbly thee desire
To commit it to the fire:
Better 'twere my Book were dead,
Than to live not perfected.

Upon Silvia, a Mistresse

When some shall say, Faire once my Silvia was;
Thou wilt complaine, False now's thy Looking-glasse:
Which renders that quite tarnisht, which was green;
And Priceless now, what Peerless once had been:
Upon thy Forme more wrinkles yet will fall,
And comming downe, shall make no noise at all.

Upon Julia's Voice

So smooth, so sweet, so silv'ry is thy voice,
As, could they hear, the Damn'd would make no noise,
But listen to thee, (walking in thy chamber)
Melting melodious words, to Lutes of Amber.

All things decay and die

All things decay with Time: The Forrest sees
The growth, and down-fall of her aged trees:
That Timber tall, which three-score *lusters* stood
The proud *Dictator* of the State-like wood:
I meane (the Soveraigne of all Plants) the Oke
Droops, dies, and falls without the cleavers stroke.

Of Love. A Sonet

How Love came in, I do not know,
Whether by th' eye, or eare, or no:
Or whether with the soule it came
(At first) infused with the same:
Whether in part 'tis here or there,
Or, like the soule, whole every where:
This troubles me: but I as well
As any other, this can tell;
That when from hence she does depart,
The out-let then is from the heart.

The Rock of Rubies: and
The quarrie of Pearls

Some ask'd me where the *Rubies* grew?
　　And nothing I did say:
But with my finger pointed to
　　The lips of *Julia.*

Some ask'd how *Pearls* did grow, and where?
   Then spoke I to my Girle,
To part her lips, and shew'd them there
   The Quarelets of Pearl.

Upon Roses ·

Under a Lawne, than skyes more cleare,
Some ruffled Roses nestling were:
And snugging there, they seem'd to lye
As in a flowrie Nunnery:
They blush'd, and look'd more fresh than flowers
Quickned of late by Pearly showers;
And all, because they were possest
But of the heat of *Julia's* breast:
Which as a warme, and moistned spring,
Gave them their ever flourishing.

The Cheat of Cupid: *Or,*
The ungentle guest

One silent night of late,
   When every creature rested,
Came one unto my gate,
   And knocking, me molested.

Who's that (said I) beats there,
   And troubles thus the Sleepie?
Cast off (said he) all feare,
   And let not Locks thus keep ye.

For I a Boy am, who
  By Moonlesse nights have swerved;
And all with showrs wet through,
  And e'en with cold half starved.

I pittifull arose,
  And soon a Taper lighted;
And did my selfe disclose
  Unto the lad benighted.

I saw he had a Bow,
  And Wings too, which did shiver;
And looking down below,
  I spy'd he had a Quiver.

I to my Chimney's shine
  Brought him, (as Love professes)
And chaf'd his hands with mine,
  And dry'd his dropping Tresses:

But when he felt him warm'd,
  Let's try this bow of ours,
And string if they be harm'd,
  Said he, with these late showrs.

Forthwith his bow he bent,
  And wedded string and arrow,
And struck me that it went
  Quite through my heart and marrow.

Then laughing loud, he flew
  Away, and thus said flying,
Adieu, mine Host, Adieu,
  Ile leave thy heart a dying.

Delight in Disorder

A sweet disorder in the dresse
Kindles in cloathes a wantonnesse:
A Lawne about the shoulders thrown
Into a fine distraction:
An erring Lace, which here and there
Enthralls the Crimson Stomacher:
A Cuffe neglectfull and thereby
Ribbands to flow confusedly:
A winning wave (deserving Note)
In the tempestuous petticote:
A carelesse shooe-string, in whose tye
I see a wilde civility:
Doe more bewitch me, than when Art
Is too precise in every part.

Upon Love

Love scorch'd my finger, but did spare
    The burning of my heart:
To signifie, in Love my share
    Sho'd be a little part.

Little I love; but if that he
    Wo'd but that heat recall:
That joynt to ashes burnt sho'd be,
    Ere I wo'd love at all.

Dean-bourn, *a rude River in* Devon, *by which sometimes he lived*

Dean-bourn, farewell; I never look to see
Deane, or thy warty incivility.
Thy rockie bottome, that doth teare thy streams,
And makes them frantick, ev'n to all extreames;
To my content, I never sho'd behold,
Were thy streames silver, or thy rocks all gold.
Rockie thou art; and rockie we discover
Thy men; and rockie are thy wayes all over.
O men, O manners; Now, and ever knowne
To be *A Rockie Generation!*
A people currish; churlish as the seas;
And rude (almost) as rudest Salvages.
With whom I did, and may re-sojourne when
Rockes turn to Rivers, Rivers turn to Men.

To Julia

How rich and pleasing thou my *Julia* art
In each thy dainty, and peculiar part!
First, for thy *Queen-ship* on thy head is set
Of flowers a sweet commingled Coronet:
About thy neck a Carkanet is bound,
Made of the *Rubie, Pearle, and Diamond*:
A golden ring, that shines upon thy thumb:
About thy wrist, the rich *Dardanium*.*

* A Bracelet, from Dardanus so call'd.

Between thy Breasts (than Doune of Swans more white)
There playes the *Saphire* with the *Chrysolite.*
No part besides must of thy selfe be known,
But by the *Topaz, Opal, Calcedon.*

To Laurels

A funerall stone,
Or Verse I covet none;
But onely crave
Of you, that I may have
A sacred Laurel springing from my grave:
Which being seen,
Blest with perpetuall greene,
May grow to be
Not so much call'd a tree,
As the eternall monument of me.

His Cavalier

Give me that man, that dares bestride
The active Sea-horse, and with pride,
Through that huge field of waters ride:
Who, with his looks too, can appease
The ruffling winds and raging Seas,
In mid'st of all their outrages.
This, this a virtuous man can doe,
Saile against Rocks, and split them too;
I! and a world of Pikes passe through.

To his Mistresse

Choose me your Valentine;
　　Next, let us marry:
Love to the death will pine,
　　If we long tarry.

Promise, and keep your vowes,
　　Or vow ye never:
Loves doctrine disallowes
　　Troth-breakers ever.

You have broke promise twice
　　(Deare) to undoe me;
If you prove faithlesse thrice,
　　None then will wooe y[e].

To the generous Reader

See, and not see; and if thou chance t'espie
Some Aberrations in my Poetry;
Wink at small faults, the greater, ne'rthelesse
Hide, and with them, their Fathers nakedness.
Let's doe our best, our Watch and Ward to keep:
Homer himself, in a long work, may sleep.

The Definition of Beauty

Beauty, no other thing is, than a Beame
Flasht out between the Middle and Extreame.

To Anthea *lying in bed*

So looks *Anthea*, when in bed she lyes,
Orecome, or halfe betray'd by Tiffanies:
Like to a Twi-light, or that simpring Dawn,
That Roses shew, when misted o're with Lawn.
Twilight is yet, till that her Lawnes give way;
Which done, that Dawne, turnes then to perfect day.

To Electra

More white than whitest Lillies far,
Or Snow, or whitest Swans you are:
More white than are the whitest Creames,
Or Moone-light tinselling the streames:
More white than *Pearls*, or *Juno's* thigh;
Or *Pelops* Arme of *Yvorie.*
True, I confesse; such Whites as these
May me delight, not fully please:
Till, like *Ixion's* Cloud you be
White, warme, and soft to lye with me.

A Country life: To his Brother,
M. Tho: Herrick

Thrice, and above, blest (my soules halfe) art thou,
    In thy both Last, and Better Vow:
Could'st leave the City, for exchange, to see
    The Countries sweet simplicity:
And it to know, and practice; with intent
    To grow the sooner innocent:
By studying to know vertue; and to aime
    More at her nature, than her name:
The last is but the least; the first doth tell
    Wayes lesse to live, than to live well:
And both are knowne to thee, who now can'st live
    Led by thy conscience; to give
Justice to soone-pleas'd nature; and to show,
    Wisdome and she together goe,
And keep one Centre: This with that conspires,
    To teach Man to confine desires:
And know, that Riches have their proper stint,
    In the contented mind, not mint.
And can'st instruct, that those who have the itch
    Of craving more, are never rich.
These things thou know'st to'th'height, and dost prevent
    That plague; because thou art content
With that Heav'n gave thee with a warie hand,
    (More blessed in thy Brasse, than Land)
To keep cheap Nature even, and upright;
    To coole, not cocker Appetite.
Thus thou can'st tearcely live to satisfie
    The belly chiefly; not the eye:

Keeping the barking stomach wisely quiet,
    Lesse with a neat, than needfull diet.
But that which most makes sweet thy country life,
    Is, the fruition of a wife:
Whom (Stars consenting with thy Fate) thou hast
    Got, not so beautifull, as chast:
By whose warme side thou dost securely sleep
    (While Love the Centinell doth keep)
With those deeds done by day, which n'er affright
    Thy silken slumbers in the night.
Nor has the darknesse power to usher in
    Feare to those sheets, that know no sin.
But still thy wife, by chast intentions led,
    Gives thee each night a Maidenhead.
The Damaskt medowes, and the peebly streames
    Sweeten, and make soft your dreames:
The Purling springs, groves, birds, and well-weav'd Bowrs,
    With fields enameled with flowers,
Present their shapes; while fantasie discloses
    Millions of *Lillies* mixt with *Roses*.
Then dream, ye heare the Lamb by many a bleat
    Woo'd to come suck the milkie Teat:
While *Faunus* in the Vision comes to keep,
    From rav'ning wolves, the fleecie sheep.
With thousand such enchanting dreams, that meet
    To make sleep not so sound, as sweet:
Nor can these figures so thy rest endeare,
    As not to rise when *Chanticlere*
Warnes the last Watch; but with the Dawne dost rise
    To work, but first to sacrifice;

Making thy peace with heav'n, for some late fault,
 With Holy-meale, and spirting-salt.
Which done, thy painfull Thumb this sentence tells us,
 Jove for our labour all things sells us.
Nor are thy daily and devout affaires
 Attended with those desp'rate cares,
Th' industrious Merchant has; who for to find
 Gold, runneth to the Western Inde,
And back again, (tortur'd with fears) doth fly,
 Untaught, to suffer Poverty.
But thou at home, blest with securest ease,
 Sitt'st, and beleev'st that there be seas,
And watrie dangers; while thy whiter hap,
 But sees these things within thy Map.
And viewing them with a more safe survey,
 Mak'st easie Feare unto thee say,
A heart thrice wall'd with Oke, and Brasse, that man
 Had, first, durst plow the Ocean.
But thou at home without or tyde or gale,
 Canst in thy Map securely saile:
Seeing those painted Countries; and so guesse
 By those fine Shades, their Substances:
And from thy Compasse taking small advice,
 Buy'st Travell at the lowest price.
Nor are thine eares so deafe, but thou canst heare
 (Far more with wonder, than with feare)
Fame tell of States, of Countries, Courts, and Kings;
 And beleeve there be such things:
When of these truths, thy happyer knowledge lyes,
 More in thine eares, than in thine eyes.

And when thou hear'st by that too-true-Report,
  Vice rules the Most, or All at Court:
Thy pious wishes are, (though thou not there)
  Vertue had, and mov'd her Sphere.
But thou liv'st fearlesse; and thy face ne'r shewes
  Fortune when she comes, or goes.
But with thy equall thoughts, prepar'd dost stand,
  To take her by the either hand:
Nor car'st which comes the first, the foule or faire;
  A wise man ev'ry way lies square.
And like a surly *Oke* with storms perplext;
  Growes still the stronger, strongly vext.
Be so, bold spirit; stand Center-like, unmov'd;
  And be not onely thought, but prov'd
To be what I report thee; and inure
  Thy selfe, if want comes to endure:
And so thou dost: for thy desires are
  Confin'd to live with private *Larr*:
Not curious whether Appetite be fed,
  Or with the first, or second bread.
Who keep'st no proud mouth for delicious cates:
  Hunger makes coorse meats, delicates.
Can'st, and unurg'd, forsake that Larded fare,
  Which Art, not Nature, makes so rare;
To taste boyl'd Nettles, Colworts, Beets, and eate
  These, and sowre herbs, as dainty meat?
While soft Opinion makes thy *Genius* say,
  Content makes all Ambrosia.
Nor is it, that thou keep'st this stricter size
  So much for want, as exercise:

To numb the sence of Dearth, which sho'd sinne haste it,
    Thou might'st but onely see't, not taste it.
Yet can thy humble roofe maintaine a Quire
    Of singing Crickits by thy fire:
And the brisk Mouse may feast her selfe with crums,
    Till that the green-ey'd Kitling comes.
Then to her Cabbin, blest she can escape
    The sudden danger of a Rape.
And thus thy little-well-kept-stock doth prove,
    Wealth cannot make a life, but Love.
Nor art thou so close-handed, but can'st spend
    (Counsell concurring with the end)
As well as spare: still conning o'r this Theame,
    To shun the first, and last extreame.
Ordaining that thy small stock find no breach,
    Or to exceed thy Tether's reach:
But to live round, and close, and wisely true
    To thine own selfe; and knowne to few.
Thus let thy Rurall Sanctuary be
    Elizium to thy wife and thee;
There to disport your selves with golden measure:
    For seldome use commends the pleasure.
Live, and live blest; thrice happy Paire; Let Breath,
    But lost to one, be th' others death.
And as there is one Love, one Faith, one Troth,
    Be so one Death, one Grave to both.
Till when, in such assurance live, ye may
    Nor feare, or wish your dying day.

Divination by a Daffadill

When a Daffadill I see,
Hanging down his head t'wards me;
Guesse I may, what I must be:
First, I shall decline my head;
Secondly, I shall be dead;
Lastly, safely buryed.

To the Painter, to draw him a Picture

Come, skilfull *Lupo*, now, and take
Thy *Bice*, thy *Umber*, *Pink*, and *Lake*;
And let it be thy Pensils strife,
To paint a Bridgeman to the life:
Draw him as like too, as you can,
An old, poore, lying, flatt'ring man:
His cheeks be-pimpled, red and blue;
His nose and lips of mulbrie hiew.
Then for an easie fansie; place
A Burling iron for his face:
Next, make his cheeks with breath to swell,
And for to speak, if possible:
But do not so; for feare, lest he
Sho'd by his breathing, poyson thee.

A Lyrick to Mirth

While the milder Fates consent,
Let's enjoy our merryment:
Drink, and dance, and pipe, and play;
Kisse our *Dollies* night and day:
Crown'd with clusters of the Vine;
Let us sit, and quaffe our wine.
Call on *Bacchus*; chaunt his praise;
Shake the *Thyrse*, and bite the *Bayes*:
Rouze *Anacreon* from the dead;
And return him drunk to bed:
Sing o're *Horace*; for ere long
Death will come and mar the song:
Then shall *Wilson* and *Gotiere**
Never sing, or play more here.

Upon Julia's *Riband*

As shews the Aire, when with a Rain-bow grac'd;
So smiles that Riband 'bout my *Julia's* waste:
Or like – Nay 'tis that *Zonulet* of love,
Wherein all pleasures of the world are wove.

* John Wilson, composer and musician; Jacques Gaultier (Gouter,
French lutanist.

The sadnesse of things for Sapho's *sicknesse*

Lillies will languish; Violets look ill;
Sickly the Prim-rose: Pale the Daffadill:
That gallant Tulip will hang down his head,
Like to a Virgin newly ravished.
Pansies will weep; and Marygolds will wither;
And keep a Fast, and Funerall together,
If *Sapho* droop; Daisies will open never,
But bid Good-night, and close their lids for ever.

The Teare sent to her from Stanes

Glide, gentle streams, and beare
Along with you my teare
        To that coy Girle;
        Who smiles, yet slayes
        Me with delayes;
And strings my tears as Pearle.

See! see she's yonder set,
Making a Carkanet
        Of Maiden-flowers!
        There, there present
        This Orient,
And Pendant Pearle of ours.

Then say, I've sent one more
Jem to enrich her store;

And that is all
Which I can send,
Or vainly spend,
For tears no more will fall.

Nor will I seek supply
Of them, the spring's once drie;
But Ile devise,
(Among the rest)
A way that's best
How I may save mine eyes.

Yet say; sho'd she condemne
Me to surrender them;
Then say; my part
Must be to weep
Out them, to keep
A poore, yet loving heart.

Say too, She wo'd have this;
She shall: Then my hope is,
That when I'm poore,
And nothing have
To send, or save;
I'm sure she'll ask no more.

Upon one Lillie, *who marryed with a maid call'd* Rose

What times of sweetnesse this faire day fore-shows,
When as the Lilly marries with the Rose!
What next is lookt for? but we all sho'd see
To spring from these a sweet Posterity.

An Epitaph upon a child

Virgins promis'd when I dy'd,
That they wo'd each Primrose-tide,
Duely, Morne and Ev'ning, come,
And with flowers dresse my Tomb.
Having promis'd, pay your debts,
Maids, and here strew Violets.

His fare-well to Sack

Farewell thou Thing, time-past so knowne, so deare
To me, as blood to life and spirit: Neare,
Nay, thou more neare than kindred, friend, man, wife,
Male to the female, soule to body: Life
To quick action, or the warme soft side
Of the resigning, yet resisting Bride.
The kisse of Virgins; First-fruits of the bed;
Soft speech, smooth touch, the lips, the Maiden-head:
These, and a thousand sweets, co'd never be
So neare, or deare, as thou wast once to me.

O thou the drink of Gods, and Angels! Wine
That scatter'st Spirit and Lust; whose purest shine,
More radiant than the Summers Sun-beams shows;
Each way illustrious, brave; and like to those
Comets we see by night; whose shagg'd portents
Fore-tell the comming of some dire events:
Or some full flame, which with a pride aspires,
Throwing about his wild, and active fires.
'Tis thou, above Nectar, O Divinest soule!
(Eternall in thy self) that canst controule
That, which subverts whole nature, grief and care;
Vexation of the mind, and damn'd Despaire.
'Tis thou, alone, who with thy Mistick Fan,
Work'st more than Wisdome, Art, or Nature can,
To rouze the sacred madnesse; and awake
The frost-bound-blood, and spirits; and to make
Them frantick with thy raptures, flashing through
The soule, like lightning, and as active too.
'Tis not *Apollo* can, or those thrice three
Castalian Sisters, sing, if wanting thee.
Horace, *Anacreon* both had lost their fame,
Had'st thou not fill'd them with thy fire and flame.
Phœbean splendour! and thou *Thespian* spring!
Of which, sweet Swans must drink, before they sing
Their true-pac'd-Numbers, and their Holy-Layes,
Which makes them worthy *Cedar*, and the *Bayes*.
But why? why longer doe I gaze upon
Thee with the eye of admiration?
Since I must leave thee; and enforc'd, must say
To all thy witching beauties, Goe, Away.
But if thy whimpring looks doe ask me why?
Then know, that Nature bids thee goe, not I.

'Tis her erroneous self has made a braine
Uncapable of such a Soveraigne,
As is thy powerfull selfe. Prethee not smile;
Or smile more inly; lest thy looks beguile
My vowes denounc'd in zeale, which thus much show
    thee,
That I have sworn, but by thy looks to know thee.
Let others drink thee freely; and desire
Thee and their lips espous'd; while I admire,
And love thee; but not taste thee. Let my Muse
Faile of thy former helps; and onely use
Her inadult'rate strength: what's done by me
Hereafter, shall smell of the Lamp, not thee.

Upon Mrs. Eliz: Wheeler,* *under the name of* Amarillis

Sweet *Amarillis*, by a Spring's
Soft and soule-melting murmurings,
Slept; and thus sleeping, thither flew
A *Robin-Red-brest*; who at view,
Not seeing her at all to stir,
Brought leaves and mosse to cover her:
But while he, perking, there did prie
About the Arch of either eye;
The lid began to let out day;
At which poore *Robin* flew away:
And seeing her not dead, but all disleav'd;
He chirpt for joy, to see himself disceav'd.

* Martha Herrick, the poet's first cousin.

The suspition upon his over-much familiarity with a Gentlewoman

And must we part, because some say,
Loud is our love, and loose our play,
And more than well becomes the day?
Alas for pitty! and for us
Most innocent, and injur'd thus.
Had we kept close, or play'd within,
Suspition now had been the sinne,
And shame had follow'd long ere this,
T'ave plagu'd, what now unpunisht is.
But we as fearlesse of the Sunne,
As faultlesse; will not wish undone,
What now is done: since *where no sin*
Unbolts the doore, no shame comes in.
Then comely and most fragrant Maid,
Be you more warie, than afraid
Of these Reports; because you see
The fairest most suspected be.
The common formes have no one eye,
Or eare of burning jealousie
To follow them: but chiefly, where
Love makes the cheek, and chin a sphere
To dance and play in: (Trust me) there
Suspicion questions every haire.
Come, you are faire; and sho'd be seen
While you are in your sprightfull green:
And what though you had been embrac't
By me, were you for that unchast?

No, no, no more than is yond' Moone,
Which shining in her perfect Noone;
In all that great and glorious light,
Continues cold, as is the night.
Then, beauteous Maid, you may retire;
And as for me, my chast desire
Shall move t'wards you; although I see
Your face no more: So live you free
From Fames black lips, as you from me.

The Curse. A Song

Goe, perjur'd man; and if thou ere return
To see the small remainders in mine Urne:
When thou shalt laugh at my Religious dust;
And ask, Where's now the colour, forme and trust
Of Womans beauty? and with hand more rude
Rifle the Flowers which the Virgins strew'd:
Know, I have pray'd to Furie, that some wind
May blow my ashes up, and strike thee blind.

The wounded Cupid. Song

Cupid as he lay among
Roses, by a Bee was stung.
Whereupon in anger flying
To his Mother, said thus crying;
Help! O help! your Boy's a dying.

C

And why, my pretty Lad, said she?
Then blubbering, replyed he,
A winged Snake has bitten me,
Which Country people call a Bee.
At which she smil'd; then with her hairs
And kisses drying up his tears:
Alas! said she, my Wag! if this
Such a pernicious torment is:
Come tel me then, how great's the smart
Of those, thou woundest with thy Dart!

The Vision

Sitting alone (as one forsook)
Close by a Silver-shedding Brook;
With hands held up to Love, I wept;
And after sorrowes spent, I slept:
Then in a Vision I did see
A glorious forme appeare to me:
A Virgins face she had; her dresse
Was like a sprightly *Spartanesse*.
A silver bow with green silk strung,
Down from her comely shoulders hung:
And as she stood, the wanton Aire
Dandled the ringlets of her haire.
Her legs were such *Diana* shows,
When tuckt up she a hunting goes;
With Buskins shortned to descrie
The happy dawning of her thigh:

Which when I saw, I made accesse
To kisse that tempting nakednesse:
But she forbad me, with a wand
Of Mirtle she had in her hand:
And chiding me, said, Hence, Remove,
Herrick, thou art too coorse to love.

Love me little, love me long

You say, to me-wards your affection's strong;
Pray love me little, so you love me long.
Slowly goes farre: The meane is best: Desire
Grown violent, do's either die, or tire.

Upon a Virgin kissing a Rose

'Twas but a single *Rose*,
    Till you on it did breathe;
But since (me thinks) it shows
    Not so much *Rose*, as Wreathe.

Upon a Wife that dyed mad with Jealousie

In this little Vault she lyes,
Here, with all her jealousies:
Quiet yet; but if ye make
Any noise, they both will wake,
And such spirits raise, 'twill then
Trouble Death to lay agen.

Upon the Bishop of Lincolne's *Imprisonment*

Never was Day so over-sick with showres,
But that it had some intermitting houres.
Never was Night so tedious, but it knew
The Last Watch out, and saw the Dawning too.
Never was Dungeon so obscurely deep,
Wherein or Light, or Day, did never peep.
Never did Moone so ebbe, or seas so wane,
But they left Hope-seed to fill up againe.
So you, my Lord, though you have now your stay,
Your Night, your Prison, and your Ebbe; you may
Spring up afresh; when all these mists are spent,
And Star-like, once more, guild our Firmament.
Let but That Mighty *Cesar* speak, and then,
All bolts, all barres, all gates shall cleave; as when
That Earth-quake shook the house, and gave the stout
Apostles, way (unshackled) to goe out.
This, as I wish for, so I hope to see;
Though you (my Lord) have been unkind to me:
To wound my heart, and never to apply
(When you had power) the meanest remedy:
Well; though my griefe by you was gall'd, the more;
Yet I bring Balme and Oile to heal your sore.

His Protestation to Perilla

Noone-day and Midnight shall at once be seene:
Trees, at one time, shall be both sere and greene:

Fire and water shall together lye
In one-self-sweet-conspiring sympathie:
Summer and Winter shall at one time show
Ripe eares of corne, and up to th'eares in snow:
Seas shall be sandlesse; Fields devoid of grasse;
Shapelesse the world (as when all *Chaos* was)
Before, my deare *Perilla*, I will be
False to my vow, or fall away from thee.

Vertue is sensible of suffering

Though a wise man all pressures can sustaine;
His vertue still is sensible of paine:
Large shoulders though he has, and well can beare,
He feeles when Packs do pinch him; and the where.

To Dianeme

Sweet, be not proud of those two eyes,
Which Star-like sparkle in their skies:
Nor be you proud, that you can see
All hearts your captives; yours, yet free:
Be you not proud of that rich haire,
Which wantons with the Love-sick aire:
When as that *Rubie*, which you weare,
Sunk from the tip of your soft eare,
Will last to be a precious Stone,
When all your world of Beautie's gone.

To a Gentlewoman objecting to him his gray haires

Am I despis'd, because you say,
And I dare sweare, that I am gray?
Know, Lady, you have but your day:
And time will come when you shall weare
Such frost and snow upon your haire:
And when (though long it comes to passe)
You question with your Looking-glasse;
And in that sincere *Christall* seek,
But find no Rose-bud in your cheek:
Nor any bed to give the shew
Where such a rare Carnation grew.
Ah! then too late, close in your chamber keeping,
                It will be told
                That you are old;
By those true teares y'are weeping.

On himselfe

I feare no Earthly Powers;
But care for crowns of flowers:
And love to have my Beard
With Wine and Oile besmear'd.
This day Ile drowne all sorrow;
Who knowes to live to morrow?

A Ring presented to Julia

Julia, I bring
To thee this Ring,
Made for thy finger fit;
To shew by this,
That our love is
(Or sho'd be) like to it.

Close though it be,
The joynt is free:
So when Love's yoke is on,
It must not gall,
Or fret at all
With hard oppression.

But it must play
Still either way;
And be, too, such a yoke,
As not too wide,
To over-slide;
Or be so strait to choak.

So we, who beare,
This beame, must reare
Our selves to such a height:
As that the stay
Of either may
Create the burden light.

And as this round
Is no where found
To flaw, or else to sever:
So let our love
As endless prove;
And pure as Gold for ever.

To the Detracter

Where others love, and praise my Verses; still
Thy long-black-Thumb-nail marks 'em out for ill:
A fellon take it, or some Whit-flaw come
For to unslate, or to untile that thumb!
But cry thee Mercy: Exercise thy nailes
To scratch or claw, so that thy tongue not railes:
Some numbers prurient are, and some of these
Are wanton with their itch; scratch, and 'twill please.

Julia's *Petticoat*

Thy Azure Robe, I did behold,
As ayrie as the leaves of gold;
Which erring here, and wandring there,
Pleas'd with transgression ev'ry where:
Sometimes 'two'd pant, and sigh, and heave,
As if to stir it scarce had leave:
But having got it; thereupon,
'Two'd make a brave expansion.

And pounc't with Stars, it shew'd to me
Like a *Celestiall Canopie.*
Sometimes 'two'd blaze, and then abate,
Like to a flame growne moderate:
Sometimes away 'two'd wildly fling;
Then to thy thighs so closely cling,
That some conceit did melt me downe,
As Lovers fall into a swoone:
And all confus'd, I there did lie
Drown'd in Delights; but co'd not die.
That Leading Cloud, I follow'd still,
Hoping t'ave seene of it my fill;
But ah! I co'd not: sho'd it move
To Life Eternal, I co'd love.

To Musick

Begin to charme, and as thou stroak'st mine eares
With thy enchantment, melt me into tears.
Then let thy active hand scu'd o're thy Lyre:
And make my spirits frantick with the fire.
That done, sink down into a silv'rie straine;
And make me smooth as Balme, and Oi[l]e againe.

Corinna's *going a Maying*

Get up, get up for shame, the Blooming Morne
Upon her wings presents the god unshorne.
  See how *Aurora* throwes her faire
  Fresh-quilted colours through the aire:
  Get up, sweet-Slug-a-bed, and see
  The Dew-bespangling Herbe and Tree.
Each Flower has wept, and bow'd toward the East,
Above an houre since; yet you not drest,
  Nay! not so much as out of bed?
  When all the Birds have Mattens seyd,
  And sung their thankfull Hymnes: 'tis sin,
  Nay, profanation to keep in,
When as a thousand Virgins on this day,
Spring, sooner than the Lark, to fetch in May.

Rise; and put on your Foliage, and be seene
To come forth, like the Spring-time, fresh and greene;
  And sweet as *Flora*. Take no care
  For Jewels for your Gowne, or Haire:
  Feare not; the leaves will strew
  Gemms in abundance upon you:
Besides, the childhood of the Day has kept,
Against you come, some *Orient Pearls* unwept:
  Come, and receive them while the light
  Hangs on the Dew-locks of the night:
  And *Titan* on the Eastern hill
  Retires himselfe, or else stands still
Till you come forth. Wash, dresse, be briefe in praying:
Few Beads are best, when once we goe a Maying.

Come, my *Corinna*, come; and comming, marke
How each field turns a street; each street a Parke
    Made green, and trimm'd with trees: see how
    Devotion gives each House a Bough,
    Or Branch: Each Porch, each doore, ere this,
    An Arke a Tabernacle is
Made up of white-thorn neatly enterwove;
As if here were those cooler shades of love.
    Can such delights be in the street,
    And open fields, and we not see't?
    Come, we'll abroad; and let's obay
    The Proclamation made for May:
And sin no more, as we have done, by staying;
But my *Corinna*, come, let's goe a Maying.

There's not a budding Boy, or Girle, this day,
But is got up, and gone to bring in May.
    A deale of Youth, ere this, is come
    Back, and with *White-thorn* laden home.
    Some have dispatcht their Cakes and Creame,
    Before that we have left to dreame:
And some have wept, and woo'd, and plighted Troth,
And chose their P[r]iest, ere we can cast off sloth:
    Many a green-gown has been given;
    Many a kisse, both odde and even:
    Many a glance too has been sent
    From out the eye, Loves Firmament:
Many a jest told of the Keyes betraying
This night, and Locks pickt, yet w'are not a Maying.

Come, let us goe, while we are in our prime;
    And take the harmlesse follie of the time.

We shall grow old apace, and die
Before we know our liberty.
Our life is short; and our dayes run
As fast away as do's the Sunne:
And as a vapour, or a drop of raine
Once lost, can ne'r be found againe:
So when or you or I are made
A fable, song, or fleeting shade;
All love, all liking, all delight
Lies drown'd with us in endlesse night.
Then while time serves, and we are but decaying;
Come, my *Corinna*, come, let's goe a Maying.

The captiv'd Bee: or,
The little Filcher

As *Julia* once a slumb'ring lay,
It chanc't a Bee did flie that way,
(After a dew, or dew-like shower)
To tipple freely in a flower.
For some rich flower, he took the lip
Of *Julia*, and began to sip;
But when he felt he suckt from thence
Hony, and in the quintessence:
He drank so much he scarce co'd stir;
So *Julia* took the Pilferer.
And thus surpriz'd (as Filchers use)
He thus began himselfe t'excuse:
Sweet *Lady-Flower*, I never brought
Hither the least one theeving thought:

But taking those rare lips of yours
For some fresh, fragrant, luscious flowers:
I thought I might there take a taste,
Where so much sirrop ran at waste.
Besides, know this, I never sting
The flower that gives me nourishing:
But with a kisse, or thanks, doe pay
For Honie, that I beare away.
This said, he laid his little *scrip*
Of hony, 'fore her Ladiship:
And told her, (as some tears did fall)
That, that he took, and that was all.
At which she smil'd; and bade him goe
And take his bag; but thus much know,
When next he came a pilfring so,
He sho'd from her full lips derive,
Hony enough to fill his hive.

An *Ode to Master* Endymion Porter, *upon his Brothers death*

Not all thy flushing Sunnes are set,
      Herrick, as yet:
Nor doth this far-drawn Hemisphere
Frown, and look sullen ev'ry where.
Daies may conclude in nights; and Suns may rest,
      As dead, within the West;
Yet the next Morne, re-guild the fragrant East.

Alas for me! that I have lost
      E'en all almost:
Sunk is my sight; set is my sun;
And all the loome of life undone:
The staffe, the Elme, the prop, the shelt'ring wall
      Whereon my Vine did crawle,
Now, now, blowne downe; needs must the old stock fall.

Yet, *Porter*, while thou keep'st alive,
      In death I thrive:
And like a *Phenix* re-aspire
From out my *Narde*, and Fun'rall fire:
And as I prune my feather'd youth, so I
      Doe mar'l how I co'd die,
When I had Thee, my chiefe Preserver, by.

I'm up, I'm up, and blesse that hand,
      Which makes me stand
Now as I doe; and but for thee,
I must confesse, I co'd not be.
The debt is paid: for he who doth resigne
      Thanks to the gen'rous Vine;
Invites fresh Grapes to fill his Presse with Wine.

To his dying Brother, *Master* William Herrick

Life of my life, take not so soone thy flight,
But stay the time till we have bade Good night.
Thou hast both Wind and Tide with thee; Thy way
As soone dispatcht is by the Night, as Day.
Let us not then so rudely henceforth goe
Till we have wept, kist, sigh't, shook hands, or so.

There's paine in parting; and a kind of hell,
When once true-lovers take their last Fare-well.
What? shall we two our endlesse leaves take here
Without a sad looke, or a solemne teare?
He knowes not Love, that hath not this truth proved,
Love is most loth to leave the thing beloved.
Pay we our Vowes, and goe; yet when we part,
Then, even then, I will bequeath my heart
Into thy loving hands: For Ile keep none
To warme my Breast, when thou my Pulse art gone.
No, here Ile last, and walk (a harmless shade)
About this Urne, wherein thy Dust is laid,
To guard it so, as nothing here shall be
Heavy, to hurt those sacred seeds of thee.

The Olive Branch

Sadly I walk't within the field,
To see what comfort it wo'd yeeld:
And as I went my private way,
An Olive-branch before me lay:
And seeing it, I made a stay.
And took it up, and view'd it; then
Kissing the *Omen*, said Amen:
Be, be it so, and let this be
A Divination unto me:
That in short time my woes shall cease;
And Love shall crown my End with Peace.

How Lillies came white

White though ye be; yet, Lillies, know,
From the first ye were not so:
　　But Ile tell ye
　　What befell ye;
Cupid and his Mother lay
In a Cloud; while both did play,
He with his pretty finger prest
The rubie niplet of her breast;
Out of the which, the creame of light,
　　Like to a Dew,
　　Fell downe on you,
　　And made ye white.

The Lilly in a Christal

You have beheld a smiling *Rose*
　　When Virgins hands have drawn
　　O'r it a Cobweb-Lawne:
And here, you see, this Lilly shows,
　　Tomb'd in a *Christal* stone,
More faire in this transparent case,
　　Than when it grew alone;
　　And had but single grace.

You see how *Creame* but naked is;
　　Nor daunces in the eye
　　Without a Strawberrie:

Or some fine tincture, like to this,
    Which draws the sight thereto,
More by that wantoning with it;
    Than when the paler hieu
    No mixture did admit.

You see how *Amber* through the streams
    More gently stroaks the sight,
    With some conceal'd delight;
Than when he darts his radiant beams
    Into the boundlesse aire:
Where either too much light his worth
    Doth all at once impaire,
    Or set it little forth.

Put Purple Grapes, or Cherries in-
    To Glasse, and they will send
    More beauty to commend
Them, from that cleane and subtile skin,
    Than if they naked stood,
And had no other pride at all,
    But their own flesh and blood,
    And tinctures naturall.

Thus Lillie, Rose, Grape, Cherry, Creame,
    And Straw-berry do stir
    More love, when they transfer
A weak, a soft, a broken beame;
    Than if they sho'd discover
At full their proper excellence;
    Without some Scean cast over,
    To juggle with the sense.

Thus let this *Christal'd Lillie* be
    A Rule, how far to teach,
    Your nakednesse must reach:
And that, no further, than we see
    Those glaring colours laid
By Arts wise hand, but to this end
    They sho'd obey a shade;
    Lest they too far extend.

So though y'are white as Swan, or Snow,
    And have the power to move
    A world of men to love:
Yet, when your Lawns and Silks shal flow;
    And that white cloud divide
Into a doubtful Twi-light; then,
    Then will your hidden Pride
    Raise greater fires in men.

To his Booke

Like to a Bride, come forth my Book, at last,
With all thy richest jewels over-cast:
Say, if there be 'mongst many jems here; one
Deservelesse of the name of *Paragon*:
Blush not at all for that; since we have set
Some *Pearls* on *Queens*, that have been counterfet.

Upon some women

Thou who wilt not love, doe this;
Learne of me what Woman is.
Something made of thred and thrumme;
A meere Botch of all and some.
Pieces, patches, ropes of haire;
In-laid Garbage ev'ry where.
Out-side silk, and out-side Lawne;
Sceanes to cheat us neatly drawne.
False in legs, and false in thighes;
False in breast, teeth, haire, and eyes:
False in head, and false enough;
Onely true in shreds and stuffe.

Impossibilities to his friend

My faithful friend, if you can see
The Fruit to grow up, or the Tree:
If you can see the colour come
Into the blushing Peare, or Plum:
If you can see the water grow
To cakes of Ice, or flakes of Snow:
If you can see, that drop of raine
Lost in the wild sea, once againe:
If you can see, how Dreams do creep
Into the Brain by easie sleep:
Then there is hope that you may see
Her love me once, who now hates me.

Faire dayes: or, *Dawnes deceitfull*

Faire was the Dawne; and but e'ne now the Skies
Shew'd like to Creame, enspir'd with Strawberries:
But on a sudden, all was chang'd and gone
That smil'd in that first-sweet complexion.
Then Thunder-claps and Lightning did conspire
To teare the world, or set it all on fire.
What trust to things below, when as we see,
As Men, the Heavens have their Hypocrisie?

To Violets

Welcome Maids of Honour,
　　　　You doe bring
　　　　In the Spring;
And wait upon her.

She has Virgins many,
　　　　Fresh and faire;
　　　　Yet you are
More sweet than any.

Y'are the Maiden Posies,
　　　　And so grac't,
　　　　To be plac't,
'Fore Damask Roses.

Yet though thus respected,
　　　　By and by
　　　　Ye doe lie,
Poore Girles, neglected.

To the Virgins, to make much of Time

Gather ye Rose-buds while ye may,
    Old Time is still a flying:
And this same flower that smiles to day,
    To morrow will be dying.

The glorious Lamp of Heaven, the Sun,
    The higher he's a getting;
The sooner will his Race be run,
    And neerer he's to Setting.

That Age is best, which is the first,
    When Youth and Blood are warmer;
But being spent, the worse, and worst
    Times, still succeed the former.

Then be not coy, but use your time;
    And while ye may, goe marry:
For having lost but once your prime,
    You may for ever tarry.

Safety to look to ones selfe

For my neighbour Ile not know,
Whether high he builds or no:
Onely this Ile look upon,
Firm be my foundation.
Sound, or unsound, let it be;
'Tis the lot ordain'd for me.
He who to the ground do's fall,
Has not whence to sink at all.

His Poetrie his Pillar

Onely a little more
  I have to write,
  Then Ile give o're,
And bid the world Good-night.

'Tis but a flying minute,
  That I must stay,
  Or linger in it;
And then I must away.

O time that cut'st down all!
  And scarce leav'st here
  Memoriall
Of any men that were.

How many lye forgot
  In Vaults beneath?
  And piece-meale rot
Without a fame in death?

Behold this living stone,
  I reare for me,
  Ne'r to be thrown
Downe, envious Time by thee.

Pillars let some set up,
  (If so they please)
  Here is my hope,
And my *Pyramides*.

The Bubble. A Song

To my revenge, and to her desp'rate feares,
Flie thou mad[d] Bubble of my sighs, and tears.
In the wild aire, when thou hast rowl'd about,
And (like a blasting Planet) found her out;
Stoop, mount, passe by to take her eye, then glare
Like to a dreadfull Comet in the Aire;
Next, when thou dost perceive her fixed sight,
For thy revenge to be most opposite;
Then like a Globe, or Ball of Wild-fire, flie,
And break thy self in shivers on her eye.

A Meditation for his Mistresse

You are a *Tulip* seen to day,
But (Dearest) of so short a stay;
That where you grew, scarce man can say.

You are a lovely *July-flower*,
Yet one rude wind, or ruffling shower,
Will force you hence, (and in an houre.)

You are a sparkling *Rose* i'th'bud,
Yet lost, ere that chast flesh and blood
Can shew where you or grew, or stood.

You are a full-spread faire-set Vine,
And can with Tendrills love intwine,
Yet dry'd, ere you distill your Wine.

You are like Balme inclosed (well)
In *Amber*, or some *Chrystall* shell,
Yet lost ere you transfuse your smell.

You are a dainty *Violet*,
Yet wither'd, ere you can be set
Within the Virgins Coronet.

You are the *Queen* all flowers among,
But die you must (faire Maid) ere long,
As He, the maker of this Song.

Lyrick for Legacies

Gold I've none, for use or show,
Neither Silver to bestow
At my death; but thus much know,
That each Lyrick here shall be
Of my love a Legacie,
Left to all posterity.
Gentle friends, then doe but please,
To accept such coynes as these;
As my last Remembrances.

To Perenna, *a Mistresse*

Deare *Perenna* prethee come,
And with *Smallage* dresse my Tomb:
Adde a *Cypresse*-sprig thereto,
With a teare; and so *Adieu*.

The Fairie Temple: or, Oberons *Chappell*.

Dedicated to Mr. John Merrifield,
Counsellor at Law

Rare Temples thou hast seen, I know,
And rich for in and outward show:
Survey this Chappell, built, alone,
Without or Lime, or Wood, or Stone:
Then say, if one th'ast seene more fine
Than this, the Fairies once, now *Thine*.

The Temple

A way enchac't with glasse and beads
There is, that to the Chappel leads:
Whose structure (for his holy rest)
Is here the *Halcion's* curious nest:
Into the which who looks shall see
His *Temple of Idolatry*:
Where he of *God-heads* has such store,
As *Rome's Pantheon* had not more.
His house of *Rimmon*, this he calls,
Girt with small bones, instead of walls.
First, in a *Neech*, more black than jet,
His Idol-Cricket there is set:
Then in a Polisht Ovall by
There stands his *Idol-Beetle-flie*:
Next in an Arch, akin to this,
His *Idol-Canker* seated is:

Then in a Round, is plac't by these,
His golden god, *Cantharides*.
So that where ere ye look, ye see,
No *Capitoll*, no *Cornish* free,
Or *Freeze*, from this fine *Fripperie*.
Now this the Fairies wo'd have known,
Theirs is a mixt Religion.
And some have heard the Elves it call
Part Pagan, part Papisticall.
If unto me all Tongues were granted,
I co'd not speak the Saints here painted.
Saint *Tit*, Saint *Nit*, Saint *Is*, Saint *Itis*,
Who 'gainst *Mabs-state* plac't here right is.
Saint *Will o'th' Wispe* (of no great bignes)
But *alias* call'd here, *Fatuus ignis*.
Saint *Frip*, Saint *Trip*, Saint *Fill*, Saint *Fillie*,
Neither those other-Saint-ships will I
Here goe about for to recite
Their number (almost) infinite,
Which one by one here set downe are
In this most curious Calendar.
First, at the entrance of the gate,
A little-Puppet-Priest doth wait,
Who squeaks to all the commers there,
Favour your tongues, who enter here.
Pure hands bring hither, without staine.
A second pules, *Hence, hence, profane.*
Hard by, i'th'shell of halfe a nut
The Holy-water there is put:
A little brush of Squirrils haires,
(Compos'd of odde, not even paires)

Stands in the Platter, or close by,
To purge the Fairie Family.
Neere to the Altar stands the Priest,
There off'ring up the Holy-Grist:
Ducking in Mood, and perfect Tense,
With (much-good-do't him) reverence.
The Altar is not here foure-square,
Nor in a forme Triangular;
Nor made of glasse, or wood, or stone,
But of a little Transverce bone;
Which boyes, and Bruckel'd* children call
(Playing for Points and Pins) *Cockall.*
Whose Linnen-Drapery is a thin
Subtile and ductile Codlin's skin:
Which o're the board is smoothly spred,
With little Seale-work Damasked.
The Fringe that circumbinds it too,
Is Spangle-work of trembling dew,
Which, gently gleaming, makes a show,
Like Frost-work glitt'ring on the Snow.
Upon this fetuous† board doth stand
Something for *Shew-bread*, and at hand
(Just in the middle of the Altar)
Upon an end, the *Fairie-Psalter,*
Grac't with the Trout-flies curious wings,
Which serve for watched‡ Ribbanings.
Now, we must know, the Elves are led
Right by the Rubrick, which they read.

* Bruckel'd = grubby (obs. dial.).
† fetuous = featous, elegant.
‡ watched (watchet) = blue-green.

And if Report of them be true,
They have their Text for what they doe;
I, and their Book of Canons too.
And, as Sir *Thomas Parson* tells,
They have their Book of Articles:
And if that Fairie Knight not lies,
They have their Book of Homilies:
And other Scriptures, that designe
A short, but righteous discipline.
The Bason stands the board upon
To take the Free-Oblation:
A little Pin-dust; which they hold
More precious, than we prize our gold:
Which charity they give to many
Poore of the Parish, (if there's any.)
Upon the ends of these neat Railes
(Hatcht, with the Silver-light of snails)
The Elves, in formall manner, fix
Two pure, and holy *Candlesticks*:
In either which a small tall bent
Burns for the Altars ornament.
For sanctity, they have, to these,
Their curious *Copes* and *Surplices*
Of cleanest *Cobweb*, hanging by
In their *Religious Vesterie*.
They have their *Ash-pans*, and their *Brooms*
To purge the Chappel and the rooms:
Their many *mumbling Masse-priests* here,
And many a dapper *Chorister*.
There ush'ring *Vergers*, here likewise,
Their *Canons*, and their *Chaunteries*:

Of *Cloyster-Monks* they have enow,
I, and their *Abby-Lubbers* too:
And if their Legend doe not lye,
They much affect the *Papacie*:
And since the last is dead, there's hope,
Elve Boniface shall next be Pope.
They have their *Cups* and *Chalices*;
Their *Pardons* and *Indulgences*:
Their *Beads* of Nits, *Bels*, *Books*, and *Wax*
Candles (forsooth) and other knacks:
Their *Holy Oyle*, their *Fasting-Spittle*;
Their *sacred Salt* here, (not a little.)
Dry *chips*, old *shooes*, *rags*, *grease*, and *bones*;
Beside their *Fumigations*,
To drive the Devill from the Cod-piece
Of the Fryar, (of work an odde-piece.)
Many a trifle too, and trinket,
And for what use, scarce man wo'd think it.
Next, then, upon the *Chanters* side
An *Apples-core* is hung up dry'd,
With ratling Kirnils, which is rung
To Call to Morn, and Even-Song.
The Saint, to which the most he prayes
And offers *Incense* Nights and dayes,
The *Lady* of the *Lobster* is,
Whose foot-pace he doth stroak and kisse;
And, humbly, chives of Saffron brings,
For his most cheerfull offerings.
When, after these, h'as paid his vows,
He lowly to the Altar bows:

And then he dons the Silk-worms shed,
(Like a *Turks Turbant* on his head)
And reverently departeth thence,
Hid in a cloud of *Frankincense*:
And by the glow-worms light wel guided,
Goes to the Feast that's now provided.

To Mistresse Katherine Bradshaw, *the lovely, that crowned him with Laurel*

My Muse in Meads has spent her many houres,
Sitting, and sorting severall sorts of flowers,
To make for others garlands; and to set
On many a head here, many a Coronet:
But, amongst All encircled here, not one
Gave her a day of Coronation;
Till you (sweet Mistresse) came and enterwove
A *Laurel* for her, (ever young as love)
You first of all crown'd her; she must of due,
Render for that, a crowne of life to you.

The Plaudite, or end of life

If after rude and boystrous seas,
My wearyed Pinnace here finds ease:
If so it be I've gain'd the shore
With safety of a faithful Ore:
If having run my Barque on ground,
Ye see the aged Vessell crown'd:

What's to be done? but on the Sands
Ye dance, and sing, and now clap hands.
The first Act's doubtfull, (but we say)
It is the last commends the Play.

To the most vertuous Mistresse Pot, who many times entertained him

When I through all my many Poems look,
And see your selfe to beautifie my Book;
Me thinks that onely lustre doth appeare
A Light ful-filling all the Region here.
Guild still with flames this Firmament, and be
A Lamp Eternall to my Poetrie.
Which if it now, or shall hereafter shine,
'Twas by your splendour (Lady) not by mine.
The Oile was yours; and that I owe for yet:
He payes the halfe, who do's confesse the Debt.

To Musique, to becalme his Fever

Charme me asleep, and melt me so
    With thy Delicious Numbers;
That being ravisht, hence I goe
    Away in easie slumbers.
        Ease my sick head,
        And make my bed,

Thou Power that canst sever
   From me this ill:
   And quickly still:
   Though thou not kill
     My Fever.

Thou sweetly canst convert the same
   From a consuming fire,
Into a gentle-licking flame,
   And make it thus expire.
    Then make me weep
    My paines asleep;
And give me such reposes,
    That I, poore I,
    May think, thereby,
    I live and die
      'Mongst Roses.

Fall on me like a silent dew,
   Or like those Maiden showrs,
Which, by the peepe of day, doe strew
   A Baptime o're the flowers.
    Melt, melt my paines,
    With thy soft straines;
That having ease me given,
    With full delight,
    I leave this light;
    And take my flight
      For Heaven.

Upon a Gentlewoman with a sweet Voice

So long you did not sing, or touch your Lute,
We knew 'twas Flesh and Blood, that there sate mute.
But when your Playing, and your Voice came in,
'Twas no more you then, but a *Cherubin*.

Upon Cupid

As lately I a Garland bound,
'Mongst Roses, I there *Cupid* found:
I took him, put him in my cup,
And drunk with Wine, I drank him up.
Hence then it is, that my poore brest
Co'd never since find any rest.

Upon Julia's *breasts*

Display thy breasts, my *Julia*, there let me
Behold that circummortall purity:
Betweene whose glories, there my lips Ile lay,
Ravisht, in that faire *Via Lactea*.

D

Best to be merry

Fooles are they, who never know
How the times away doe goe:
But for us, who wisely see
Where the bounds of black Death be:
Let's live merrily, and thus
Gratifie the *Genius*.

The Changes to Corinna

Be not proud, but now encline
Your soft eare to Discipline.
You have changes in your life,
Sometimes peace, and sometimes strife:
You have ebbes of face and flowes,
As your health or comes, or goes;
You have hopes, and doubts, and feares
Numberlesse, as are your haires.
You have Pulses that doe beat
High, and passions lesse of heat.
You are young, but must be old,
And, to these, ye must be told,
Time, ere long, will come and plow
Loathed Furrowes in your brow:
And the dimnesse of your eye
Will no other thing imply,
      But you must die
      As well as I.

To the Rose. Song

Goe happy Rose, and enterwove
With other Flowers, bind my Love.
    Tell her too, she must not be,
    Longer flowing, longer free,
    That so oft has fetter'd me.

Say (if she's fretfull) I have bands
Of Pearle, and Gold, to bind her hands:
    Tell her, if she struggle still,
    I have Mirtle rods, (at will)
    For to tame, though not to kill.

Take thou my blessing, thus, and goe,
And tell her this, but doe not so,
    Lest a handsome anger flye,
    Like a Lightning, from her eye,
    And burn thee' up, as well as I.

To Musick, to becalme a sweet-sick-youth

Charmes, that call down the moon from out her sphere,
On this sick youth work your enchantments here:
Bind up his senses with your numbers, so,
As to entrance his paine, or cure his woe.
Fall gently, gently, and a while him keep
Lost in the civill Wildernesse of sleep:
That done, then let him, dispossest of paine,
Like to a slumbring Bride, awake againe.

The comming of good luck

So Good-luck came, and on my roofe did light,
Like noyse-lesse Snow; or as the dew of night:
Not all at once, but gently, as the trees
Are, by the Sun-beams, tickel'd by degrees.

The Present: or, *The Bag of the Bee*

Fly to my Mistresse, pretty pilfring Bee,
And say, thou bring'st this Hony-bag from me:
When on her lip, thou hast thy sweet dew plac't,
Mark, if her tongue, but slily, steale a taste.
If so, we live; if not, with mournfull humme,
Tole forth my death; next, to my buryall come.

On Love

Love bade me aske a gift,
    And I no more did move,
But this, that I might shift
    Still with my clothes, my Love:
That favour granted was;
    Since which, though I love many,
Yet so it comes to passe,
    That long I love not any.

The Hock-Cart, or Harvest Home:
To the Right Honourable,
Mildmay, Earle of
Westmorland

Come Sons of Summer, by whose toile,
We are the Lords of Wine and Oile:
By whose tough labours, and rough hands,
We rip up first, then reap our lands.
Crown'd with the eares of corne, now come,
And, to the Pipe, sing Harvest home.
Come forth, my Lord, and see the Cart
Drest up with all the Country Art.
See, here a *Maukin*, there a sheet,
As spotlesse pure, as it is sweet:
The Horses, Mares, and frisking Fillies,
(Clad, all, in Linnen, white as Lillies.)
The Harvest Swaines, and Wenches bound
For joy, to see the *Hock-cart* crown'd.
About the Cart, heare, how the Rout
Of Rurall Younglings raise the shout;
Pressing before, some coming after,
Those with a shout, and these with laughter.
Some blesse the Cart; some kisse the sheaves;
Some prank them up with Oaken leaves:
Some crosse the Fill-horse*; some with great
Devotion, stroak the home-borne wheat:
While other Rusticks, lesse attent
To Prayers, than to Merryment,
Run after with their breeches rent.

* Get across (astride) the shaft horse.

Well, on, brave boyes, to your Lords Hearth,
Glitt'ring with fire; where, for your mirth,
Ye shall see first the large and cheefe
Foundation of your Feast, Fat Beefe:
With Upper Stories, Mutton, Veale
And Bacon, (which makes full the meale)
With sev'rall dishes standing by,
As here a Custard, there a Pie,
And here all tempting Frumentie.
And for to make the merry cheere,
If smirking Wine be wanting here,
There's that, which drowns all care, stout Beere;
Which freely drink to your Lords health,
Then to the Plough, (the Common-wealth)
Next to your Flailes, your Fanes, your Fatts;
Then to the Maids with Wheaten Hats:
To the rough Sickle, and crookt Sythe,
Drink frollick boyes, till all be blythe.
Feed, and grow fat; and as ye eat,
Be mindfull, that the lab'ring Neat
(As you) may have their fill of meat.
And know, besides, ye must revoke
The patient Oxe unto the Yoke,
And all goe back unto the Plough
And Harrow, (though they'r hang'd up now.)
And, you must know, your Lords word's true,
Feed him ye must, whose food fils you.
And that this pleasure is like raine,
Not sent ye for to drowne your paine,
But for to make it spring againe.

Not to love

He that will not love, must be
My Scholar, and learn this of me:
There be in Love as many feares,
As the Summers Corne has eares:
Sighs, and sobs, and sorrowes more
Than the sand, that makes the shore:
Freezing cold, and firie heats,
Fainting swoones, and deadly sweats;
Now an Ague, then a Fever,
Both tormenting Lovers ever.
Wods't thou know, besides all these,
How hard a woman 'tis to please?
How crosse, how sullen, and how soone
She shifts and changes like the Moone.
How false, how hollow she's in heart;
And how she is her owne least part:
How high she's priz'd, and worth but small;
Little thou't love, or not at all.

To Musick. A Song

Musick, thou *Queen of Heaven*, Care-charming-spel,
    That strik'st a stilnesse into hell:
Thou that tam'st *Tygers*, and fierce storms (that rise)
    With thy soule-melting Lullabies:
Fall down, down, down, from those thy chiming spheres,
To charme our soules, as thou enchant'st our eares.

Upon the death of his Sparrow.
An Elegie

Why doe not all fresh maids appeare
To work Love's Sampler onely here,
Where spring-time smiles throughout the yeare?
Are not here *Rose-buds*, *Pinks*, all flowers,
Nature begets by th' Sun and showers,
Met in one Hearce-cloth, to ore-spred
The body of the under-dead?
Phill, the late dead, the late dead Deare,
O! may no eye distill a Teare
For you once lost, who weep not here!
Had *Lesbia* (too-too-kind) but known
This Sparrow, she had scorn'd her own:
And for this dead which under-lies,
Wept out her heart, as well as eyes.
But endlesse Peace, sit here, and keep
My *Phill*, the time he has to sleep,
And thousand Virgins come and weep,
To make these flowrie Carpets show
Fresh, as their blood; and ever grow,
Till passengers shall spend their doome,
Not *Virgil's* Gnat had such a Tomb.

To Primroses fill'd with morning-dew

Why doe ye weep, sweet Babes? can Tears
    Speake griefe in you,
    Who were but borne
   Just as the modest Morne
   Teem'd her refreshing dew?
 Alas you have not known that shower,
    That marres a flower;
    Nor felt th'unkind
   Breath of a blasting wind;
   Nor are ye worne with yeares;
    Or warpt, as we,
   Who think it strange to see,
Such pretty flowers, (like to Orphans young)
To speak by Teares, before ye have a Tongue.

Speak, whim'pring Younglings, and make known
    The reason, why
    Ye droop, and weep;
   Is it for want of sleep?
   Or childish Lullabie?
 Or that ye have not seen as yet
    The *Violet?*
    Or brought a kisse
   From that Sweet-heart, to this?
   No, no, this sorrow shown
    By your teares shed,
   Wo'd have this Lecture read,
That things of greatest, so of meanest worth,
Conceiv'd with grief are, and with teares brought forth.

How Roses came red

Roses at first were white,
   Till they co'd not agree,
Whether my *Sapho's* breast,
   Or they more white sho'd be.

But being vanquisht quite,
   A blush their cheeks bespred;
Since which (beleeve the rest)
   The *Roses* first came red.

How Violets came blew

Love on a day (wise Poets tell)
   Some time in wrangling spent,
Whether the Violets sho'd excell,
   Or she, in sweetest scent.

But *Venus* having lost the day,
   Poore Girles, she fell on you
And beat ye so, (as some dare say)
   Her blowes did make ye blew.

To the Willow-tree

Thou art to all lost love the best,
   The onely true plant found,
Wherewith young men and maids distrest,
   And left of love, are crown'd.

When once the Lovers Rose is dead,
 Or laid aside forlorne;
Then Willow-garlands, 'bout the head,
 Bedew'd with teares, are worne.

When with Neglect, (the Lovers bane)
 Poore Maids rewarded be,
For their love lost; their onely gaine
 Is but a Wreathe from thee.

And underneath thy cooling shade,
 (When weary of the light)
The love-spent Youth, and love-sick Maid,
 Come to weep out the night.

Mrs. Eliz. Wheeler, *under the name of the lost Shepardesse*

Among the *Mirtles*, as I walkt,
Love and my sighs thus intertalkt:
Tell me, said I, in deep distresse,
Where I may find my Shepardesse.
Thou foole, said Love, know'st thou not this?
In every thing that's sweet, she is.
In yond' *Carnation* goe and seek,
There thou shalt find her lip and cheek:
In that ennamel'd *Pansie* by,
There thou shalt have her curious eye:
In bloome of *Peach*, and *Roses* bud,
There waves the Streamer of her blood.

'Tis true, said I, and thereupon
I went to pluck them one by one,
To make of parts an union;
But on a sudden all were gone.
At which I stopt; Said Love, these be
The true resemblances of thee;
For as these flowers, thy joyes must die,
And in the turning of an eye;
And all thy hopes of her must wither,
Like those short sweets ere knit together.

To Anthea, *who may command him any thing*

Bid me to live, and I will live
    Thy Protestant to be:
Or bid me love, and I will give
    A loving heart to thee.

A heart as soft, a heart as kind,
    A heart as sound and free,
As in the whole world thou canst find,
    That heart Ile give to thee.

Bid that heart stay, and it will stay,
    To honour thy Decree:
Or bid it languish quite away,
    And't shall doe so for thee.

Bid me to weep, and I will weep,
    While I have eyes to see:
And having none, yet I will keep
    A heart to weep for thee.

Bid me despaire, and Ile despaire,
    Under that *Cypresse* tree:
Or bid me die, and I will dare
    E'en Death, to die for thee.

Thou art my life, my love, my heart,
    The very eyes of me:
And hast command of every part,
    To live and die for thee.

To Meddowes

Ye have been fresh and green,
    Ye have been fill'd with flowers:
And ye the Walks have been
    Where Maids have spent their houres.

You have beheld, how they
    With *Wicker Arks* did come
To kisse, and beare away
    The richer Couslips home.

Y'ave heard them sweetly sing,
    And seen them in a Round:
Each Virgin, like a Spring,
    With Hony-succles crown'd.

But now, we see, none here,
    Whose silv'rie feet did tread,
And with dishevell'd Haire,
    Adorn'd this smoother Mead.

Like Unthrifts, having spent,
    Your stock, and needy grown,
Y'are left here to lament
    Your poore estates, alone.

Miseries

Though hourely comforts from the Gods we see,
No life is yet life-proofe from miserie.

To the Yew and Cypresse to grace his Funerall

Both you two have
Relation to the grave:
    And where
The *Fun'rall-Trump* sounds, you are there.

I shall be made
Ere long a fleeting shade:
    Pray come,
And doe some honour to my Tomb.

Do not deny
My last request; for I
    Will be
Thankfull to you, or friends, for me.

A Nuptiall Song, or Epithalamie, on Sir Clipseby Crew and his Lady

What's that we see from far? the spring of Day
Bloom'd from the East, or faire Injewel'd May
    Blowne out of April; or some New-
    Star fill'd with glory to our view,
        Reaching at heaven,
To adde a nobler Planet to the seven?
    Say, or doe we not descrie
Some Goddesse, in a cloud of Tiffanie
      To move, or rather the
    Emergent *Venus* from the Sea?

'Tis she! 'tis she! or else some more Divine
Enlightned substance; mark how from the Shrine
    Of holy Saints she paces on,
    Treading upon *Vermilion*
        And *Amber*; Spice-
ing the Chafte Aire with fumes of Paradise.
    Then come on, come on, and yeeld
A savour like unto a blessed field,
      When the bedabled Morne
    Washes the golden eares of corne.

See where she comes; and smell how all the street
Breathes Vine-yards and Pomgranats: O how sweet!
    As a fir'd Altar, is each stone,
    Perspiring pounded Cynamon.
      The Phenix nest,
Built up of odours, burneth in her breast.

Who therein wo'd not consume
His soule to Ash-heaps in that rich perfume?
    Bestroaking Fate the while
He burnes to Embers on the Pile.

Himen, O Himen! Tread the sacred ground;
Shew thy white feet, and head with Marjoram crown'd:
    Mount up thy flames, and let thy Torch
    Display the Bridegroom in the porch,
        In his desires
More towring, more disparkling than thy fires:
    Shew her how his eyes do turne
And roule about, and in their motions burne
        Their balls to Cindars: haste,
Or else to ashes he will waste.

Glide by the banks of Virgins then, and passe
The Shewers of Roses, lucky-foure-leav'd grasse:
    The while the cloud of younglings sing,
    And drown yee with a flowrie Spring:
        While some repeat
Your praise, and bless you, sprinkling you with Wheat:
    While that others doe divine;
Blest is the Bride, on whom the Sun doth shine;
        And thousands gladly wish
You multiply, as doth a Fish.

And beautious Bride we do confess y'are wise,
In dealing forth these bashfull jealousies:
    In Lov's name do so; and a price
    Set on your selfe, by being nice:

But yet take heed;
What now you seem, be not the same indeed,
And turne *Apostate*: Love will
Part of the way be met; or sit stone-still.
On then, and though you slow-
ly go, yet, howsoever, go.

And now y'are enter'd; see the Codled Cook
Runs from his *Torrid Zone*, to prie, and look,
And blesse his dainty Mistresse: see,
The Aged point out, This is she,
Who now must sway
The House (Love shield her) with her Yea and Nay:
And the smirk Butler thinks it
Sin, in's Nap'rie, not to express his wit;
Each striving to devise
Some gin, wherewith to catch your eyes.

To bed, to bed, kind Turtles, now, and write
This the short'st day, and this the longest night;
But yet too short for you: 'tis we,
Who count this night as long as three,
Lying alone,
Telling the Clock strike Ten, Eleven, Twelve, One.
Quickly, quickly then prepare;
And let the Young-men and the Bride-maids share
Your Garters; and their joynts
Encircle with the Bride-grooms Points.

By the Brides eyes, and by the teeming life
Of her green hopes, we charge ye, that no strife,

(Farther than Gentlenes tends) gets place
  Among ye, striving for her lace:
        O doe not fall
Foule in these noble pastimes, lest ye call
  Discord in, and so divide
The youthfull Bride-groom, and the fragrant Bride:
      Which Love fore-fend; but spoken,
    Be't to your praise, no peace was broken.

Strip her of Spring-time, tender-whimpring-maids,
Now *Autumne*'s come, when all those flowrie aids
  Of her Delayes must end; Dispose
    That *Lady-smock*, that *Pansie*, and that *Rose*
      Neatly apart;
But for *Prick-madam*, and for *Gentle-heart*;
    And soft-*Maidens-blush*, the Bride
Makes holy these, all others lay aside:
        Then strip her, or unto her
    Let him come, who dares undo her.

And to enchant yee more, see every where
About the Roofe a *Syren* in a Sphere;
  (As we think) singing to the dinne
  Of many a warbling *Cherubi[n]*:
      O marke yee how
The soule of Nature melts in numbers: now
    See, a thousand *Cupids* flye,
To light their Tapers at the Brides bright eye.
      To Bed; or her they'l tire,
    Were she an Element of fire.

And to your more bewitching, see, the proud
Plumpe Bed beare up, and swelling like a cloud,
    Tempting the two too modest; can
    Yee see it brusle like a Swan,
        And you be cold
To meet it, when it woo's and seemes to fold
    The Armes to hugge it? throw, throw
Your selves into the mighty over-flow
        Of that white Pride, and Drowne
    The night, with you, in floods of Downe.

The bed is ready, and the maze of Love
Lookes for the treaders; every where is wove
    Wit and new misterie; read, and
    Put in practise, to understand
        And know each wile,
Each hieroglyphick of a kisse or smile;
    And do it to the full; reach
High in your own conceit, and some way teach
        Nature and Art, one more
    Play, than they ever knew before.

If needs we must for Ceremonies-sake,
Blesse a *Sack-posset*; Luck go with it; take
    The Night-Charme quickly; you have spells,
    And magicks for to end, and hells,
        To passe; but such
And of such Torture as no one would grutch
    To live therein for ever: Frie
And consume, and grow again to die,
        And live, and in that case,
    Love the confusion of the place.

But since It must be done, dispatch, and sowe
Up in a sheet your Bride, and what if so
  It be with Rock, or walles of Brasse,
  Ye Towre her up, as *Danae* was;
    Thinke you that this,
Or hell it selfe a powerfull Bulwarke is?
  I tell yee no; but like a
Bold bolt of thunder he will make his way,
   And rend the cloud, and throw
  The sheet about, like flakes of snow.

All now is husht in silence; *Midwife-moone*,
With all her *Owle-ey'd* issue begs a boon
  Which you must grant; that's entrance; with
  Which extract, all we can call pith
    And quintiscence
Of Planetary bodies; so commence
  All faire *Constellations*
Looking upon yee, that two Nations
   Springing from two such Fires,
  May blaze the vertue of their Sires.

No fault in women

No fault in women to refuse
The offer, which they most wo'd chuse.
No fault in women, to confesse
How tedious they are in their dresse.
No fault in women, to lay on
The tincture of *Vermillion*:

And there to give the cheek a die
Of white, where nature doth deny.
No fault in women, to make show
Of largeness, when th'are nothing so:
(When true it is, the out-side swels
With inward Buckram, little else.)
No fault in women, though they be
But seldome from suspition free:
No fault in womankind, at all,
If they but slip, and never fall.

Oberons *Feast*

Shapcot! To thee the Fairy State
I with discretion, dedicate.
Because thou prizest things that are
Curious, and un-familiar.
Take first the feast; these dishes gone;
Wee'l see the Fairy-Court *anon.*

A little mushroome table spred,
After short prayers, they set on bread;
A Moon-parcht grain of purest wheat,
With some small glit'ring gritt, to eate
His choyce bitts with; then in a trice
They make a feast lesse great than nice.
But all this while his eye is serv'd,
We must not thinke his eare was sterv'd:
But that there was in place to stir
His Spleen, the chirring Grashopper;

The merry Cricket, puling Flie,
The piping Gnat for minstralcy.
And now, we must imagine first,
The Elves present to quench his thirst
A pure seed-Pearle of Infant dew,
Brought and besweetned in a blew
And pregnant violet; which done,
His kitling eyes begin to runne
Quite through the table, where he spies
The hornes of paperie Butterflies,
Of which he eates, and tastes a little
Of that we call the Cuckoes spittle.
A little Fuz-ball-pudding stands
By, yet not blessed by his hands,
That was too coorse; but then forthwith
He ventures boldly on the pith
Of sugred Rush, and eates the sagge
And well bestrutted Bees sweet bagge:
Gladding his pallat with some store
Of Emits eggs; what wo'd he more?
But Beards of Mice, a Newt's stew'd thigh,
A bloated Earewig, and a Flie;
With the Red-capt worme, that's shut
Within the concave of a Nut,
Browne as his Tooth. A little Moth,
Late fatned in a piece of cloth:
With withered cherries; Mandrakes eares;
Moles eyes; to these, the slain-Stags teares:
The unctuous dewlaps of a Snaile;
The broke-heart of a Nightingale

Ore-come in musicke; with a wine,
Ne're ravisht from the flattering Vine,
But gently prest from the soft side
Of the most sweet and dainty Bride,
Brought in a dainty daizie, which
He fully quaffs up to bewitch
His blood to height; this done, commended
Grace by his Priest; *The feast is ended.*

Event of things not in our power

By Time, and Counsell, doe the best we can,
Th'event is never in the power of man.

The Bell-man

From noise of Scare-fires rest ye free,
From Murders *Benedicitie.*
From all mischances, that may fright
Your pleasing slumbers in the night:
Mercie secure ye all, and keep
The Goblin from ye, while ye sleep.
Past one aclock, and almost two,
My Masters all, *Good day to you.*

On himselfe

Here down my wearyed limbs Ile lay;
My Pilgrims staffe; my weed of gray:
My Palmers hat; my Scallops shell;
My Crosse; my Cord; and all farewell.
For having now my journey done,
(Just at the setting of the Sun)
Here I have found a Chamber fit,
(God and good friends be thankt for it)
Where if I can a lodger be
A little while from Tramplers free;
At my up-rising next, I shall,
If not requite, yet thank ye all.
Meane while, the *Holy-Rood* hence fright
The fouler Fiend, and evill Spright,
From scaring you or yours this night.

Upon a child that dyed

Here she lies, a pretty bud,
Lately made of flesh and blood:
Who, as soone, fell fast asleep,
As her little eyes did peep.
Give her strewings; but not stir
The earth, that lightly covers her.

Content, not cates

'Tis not the food, but the content
That makes the Tables merriment.
Where Trouble serves the board, we eate
The Platters there, as soone as meat.
A little Pipkin with a bit
Of Mutton, or of Veale in it,
Set on my Table, (Trouble-free)
More than a Feast contenteth me.

To Daffadills

Faire Daffadills, we weep to see
    You haste away so soone:
As yet the early-rising Sun
    Has not attain'd his Noone.
        Stay, stay,
    Untill the hasting day
        Has run
    But to the Even-song;
And, having pray'd together, we
    Will goe with you along.

We have short time to stay, as you,
    We have as short a Spring;
As quick a growth to meet Decay,
    As you, or any thing.

We die,
As your hours doe, and drie
Away,
Like to the Summers raine;
Or as the pearles of Mornings dew
Ne'r to be found againe.

Upon a Lady that dyed in child-bed, and left a daughter behind her

As Gilly flowers do but stay
To blow, and seed, and so away;
So you sweet Lady (sweet as May)
The gardens-glory liv'd a while,
To lend the world your scent and smile.
But when your own faire print was set
Once in a Virgin *Flosculet*,
(Sweet as your selfe, and newly blown)
To give that life, resign'd your own:
But so, as still the mothers power
Lives in the pretty Lady-flower.

A New-yeares gift sent to Sir Simeon Steward

No newes of Navies burnt at Seas;
No noise of late spawn'd *Tittyries*:*
No closset plot, or open vent,
That frights men with a Parliament:

* *Tittyries* = members, so styled, of a gang of upper-class delinquents, who were in the news in December 1623.

No new devise, or late found trick,
To read by th' Starres, the Kingdoms sick:
No ginne to catch the State, or wring
The free-born Nosthrills of the King,
We send to you; but here a jolly
Verse crown'd with *Yvie*, and with *Holly*:
That tels of Winters Tales and Mirth,
That Milk-maids make about the hearth,
Of Christmas sports, the *Wassell-boule*,
That['s] tost up, after *Fox-i'th'hole*:
Of *Blind-man-buffe*, and of the care
That young men have to shooe the *Mare*:
Of Twelf-tide Cakes, of Pease, and Beanes
Wherewith ye make those merry Sceanes,
When as ye chuse your King and Queen,
And cry out, *Hey, for our town green*.
Of Ash-heapes, in the which ye use
Husbands and Wives by streakes to chuse:
Of crackling Laurrell, which fore-sounds,
A Plentious harvest to your grounds:
Of these, and such like things, for shift,
We send in stead of New-yeares gift.
Read then, and when your faces shine
With bucksome meat and capring Wine:
Remember us in Cups full crown'd,
And let our Citie-health go round,
Quite through the young maids and the men,
To the ninth number, if not tenne;
Untill the fired Chesnuts leape
For joy, to see the fruits ye reape,

From the plumpe Challice, and the Cup,
That tempts till it be tossed up:
Then as ye sit about your embers,
Call not to mind those fled Decembers;
But think on these, that are t'appeare,
As Daughters to the instant yeare:
Sit crown'd with Rose-buds, and carouse,
Till *Liber Pater* twirles the house
About your eares; and lay upon
The yeare (your cares) that's fled and gon.
And let the russet Swaines the Plough
And Harrow hang up resting now;
And to the Bag-pipe all addresse;
Till sleep takes place of wearinesse.
And thus, throughout, with Christmas playes
Frolick the full twelve Holy-dayes.

The Christian Militant

A man prepar'd against all ills to come,
That dares to dead the fire of martirdome:
That sleeps at home; and sayling there at ease,
Feares not the fierce sedition of the Seas:
That's counter-proofe against the Farms mis-haps,
Undreadfull too of courtly thunderclaps:
That weares one face (like heaven) and never showes
A change, when Fortune either comes, or goes:
That keepes his own strong guard, in the despight
Of what can hurt by day, or harme by night:
That takes and re-delivers every stroake
Of Chance, (as made up all of rock, and oake:)

That sighs at others death; smiles at his own
Most dire and horrid crucifixion.
Who for true glory suffers thus; we grant
Him to be here our *Christian militant*.

The Kisse. *A Dialogue*

1. Among thy Fancies, tell me this,
   What is the thing we call a kisse?
2. I shall resolve ye, what it is.

   It is a creature born and bred
   Between the lips, (all cherrie-red,)
   By love and warme desires fed,
Chor. And makes more soft the Bridall Bed.

2. It is an active flame, that flies,
   First, to the Babies of the eyes;
   And charmes them there with lullabies;
Chor. And stils the Bride too, when she cries.

2. Then to the chin, the cheek, the eare,
   It frisks, and flyes, now here, now there,
   'Tis now farre off, and then tis nere;
Chor. And here, and there, and every where.

1. Ha's it a speaking virtue? 2. Yes;
1. How speaks it, say? 2. Do you but this,
   Part your joyn'd lips, then speaks your kisse;
Chor. And this loves sweetest language is.

1. Has it a body? 2. I, and wings
   With thousand rare encolourings:
   And as it flyes, it gently sings,
Chor. Love, honie yeelds; but never stings.

To his honoured kinsman Sir William
Soame. *Epig.*

I can but name thee, and methinks I call
All that have been, or are canonicall
For love and bountie, to come neare, and see,
Their many vertues volum'd up in thee;
In thee Brave Man! Whose incorrupted fame,
Casts forth a light like to a Virgin flame:
And as it shines, it throwes a scent about,
As when a Rain-bow in perfumes goes out.
So vanish hence, but leave a name, as sweet,
As *Benjamin*, and *Storax*, when they meet.

To Larr

No more shall I, since I am driven hence,
Devote to thee my graines of Frankinsence:
No more shall I from mantle-trees hang downe,
To honour thee, my little Parsly crown:
No more shall I (I feare me) to thee bring
My chives of Garlick for an offering:
No more shall I, from henceforth, heare a quire
Of merry Crickets by my Country fire,
Go where I will, thou luckie *Larr* stay here,
Warme by a glit'ring chimnie all the yeare.

His age, dedicated to his peculiar friend, M. John
Wickes, *under the name of* Posthumus

Ah *Posthumus*! Our yeares hence flye,
And leave no sound; nor piety,
   Or prayers, or vow
Can keepe the wrinkle from the brow:
   But we must on,
As Fate do's lead or draw us; none,
None, *Posthumus*, co'd ere decline
The doome of cruell *Proserpine*.

The pleasing wife, the house, the ground
Must all be left, no one plant found
   To follow thee,
Save only the *Curst-Cipresse* tree:
   A merry mind
Looks forward, scornes what's left behind:
Let's live, my *Wickes*, then, while we may,
And here enjoy our Holiday.

W'ave seen the past-best Times, and these
Will nere return, we see the Seas,
   And Moons to wain;
But they fill up their Ebbs again:
   But vanisht man,
Like to a Lilly-lost, nere can,
Nere can repullulate, or bring
His dayes to see a second Spring.

But on we must, and thither tend,
Where *Anchus* and rich *Tullus* blend
      Their sacred seed:
Thus has *Infernall Jove* decreed;
        We must be made,
Ere long, a song, ere long, a shade.
Why then, since life to us is short,
Lets make it full up, by our sport.

Crown we our Heads with Roses then,
And 'noint with *Tirian Balme*; for when
      We two are dead,
The world with us is buried.
        Then live we free,
As is the Air, and let us be
Our own fair wind, and mark each one
Day with the white and Luckie stone.

We are not poore; although we have
No roofs of Cedar, nor our brave
      Baiæ, nor keep
Account of such a flock of sheep;
        Nor Bullocks fed
To lard the shambles: Barbels bred
To kisse our hands, nor do we wish
For *Pollio's* Lampries in our dish.

If we can meet, and so conferre,
Both by a shining Salt-seller;
        And have our Roofe,
Although not archt, yet weather proofe,
        And seeling free,

From that cheape *Candle baudery*:*
We'le eate our Beane with that full mirth,
As we were Lords of all the earth.

Well then, on what Seas we are tost,
Our comfort is, we can't be lost.
   Let the winds drive
Our Barke; yet she will keepe alive
   Amidst the deepes;
'Tis constancy (my *Wickes*) which keepes
The Pinnace up; which though she erres
I'th' Seas, she saves her passengers.

Say, we must part (sweet mercy blesse
Us both i'th' Sea, Camp, Wildernesse)
   Can we so farre
Stray, to become lesse circular,†
   Than we are now?
No, no, that selfe same heart, that vow,
Which made us one, shall ne'r undoe;
Or ravell so, to make us two.

Live in thy peace; as for my selfe,
When I am bruised on the Shelfe
   Of Time, and show
My locks behung with frost and snow:
   When with the reume,
The cough, the ptisick, I consume
Unto an almost nothing; then,
The Ages fled, Ile call agen:

* *Baudery* = dirt (here, soot stains, etc.).
† Circular = complete, at one.

And with a teare compare these last
Lame, and bad times, with those are past,
  While *Baucis* by,
My old leane wife, shall kisse it dry:
  And so we'l sit
By'th'fire, foretelling snow and slit,
And weather by our aches, grown
Now old enough to be our own

True Calenders, as Pusses eare
Washt ore 's to tell what change is neare:
  Then to asswage
The gripings of the chine by age,
   I'le call my young
Iülus to sing such a song
I made upon my *Julia's* brest;
And of her blush at such a feast.

Then shall he read that flowre of mine
Enclos'd within a christall shrine:
  A Primrose next;
A piece, then of a higher text:
  For to beget
In me a more transcendant heate,
Than that insinuating fire,
Which crept into each aged Sire

When the faire *Hellen*, from her eyes,
Shot forth her loving Sorceries:
  At which I'le reare
Mine aged limbs above my chaire:

And hearing it,
Flutter and crow, as in a fit
Of fresh concupiscence, and cry,
No lust theres like to Poetry.

Thus frantick crazie man (God wot)
Ile call to mind things half forgot:
             And oft between,
Repeat the Times that I have seen!
             Thus ripe with tears,
And twisting my *Iülus* hairs;
Doting, Ile weep and say (In Truth)
Baucis, these were my sins of youth.

Then next Ile cause my hopefull Lad
(If a wild Apple can be had)
             To crown the Hearth,
(*Larr* thus conspiring with our mirth)
             Then to infuse
Our browner Ale into the cruse:
Which sweetly spic't, we'l first carouse
Unto the *Genius* of the house.

Then the next health to friends of mine
(Loving the brave *Burgundian wine*)
             High sons of Pith,
Whose fortunes I have frolickt with:
             Such as co'd well
Bear up the Magick bough, and spel:
And dancing 'bout the Mystick *Thyrse*,
Give up the just applause to verse:

To those, and then agen to thee
We'l drink, my *Wickes*, untill we be
Plump as the cherry,
Though not so fresh, yet full as merry
As the crickit;
The untam'd Heifer, or the Pricket,
Untill our tongues shall tell our ears,
W'are younger by a score of years.

Thus, till we see the fire lesse shine
From th' embers, than the kitlings eyne,
We'l still sit up,
Sphering about the wassail cup,
To all those times,
Which gave me honour for my Rhimes,
The cole once spent, we'l then to bed,
Farre more than night bewearied.

Her Bed

See'st thou that Cloud as silver cleare,
Plump, soft, and swelling every where?
Tis *Julia's* Bed, and she sleeps there.

The meddow verse or Aniversary to *Mistris* Bridget Lowman

Come with the Spring-time, forth Fair Maid, and be
This year again, the *medows Deity*.
Yet ere ye enter, give us leave to set
Upon your Head this flowry Coronet:

To make this neat distinction from the rest;
You are the Prime, and Princesse of the Feast:
To which, with silver feet lead you the way,
While sweet-breath Nimphs, attend on you this Day.
This is your houre; and best you may command,
Since you are Lady of this Fairie land.
Full mirth wait on you; and such mirth as shall
Cherrish the cheek, but make none blush at all.

The parting verse, the feast there ended

Loth to depart, but yet at last, each one
Back must now go to's habitation:
Not knowing thus much, when we once do sever,
Whether or no, that we shall meet here ever.
As for my self, since time a thousand cares
And griefs hath fil'de upon my silver hairs;
'Tis to be doubted whether I next yeer,
Or no, shall give ye a re-meeting here.
If die I must, then my last vow shall be,
You'l with a tear or two, remember me,
Your sometime Poet; but if fates do give
Me longer date, and more fresh springs to live:
Oft as your field, shall her old age renew,
Herrick shall make the meddow-verse for you.

Chop-Cherry

Thou gav'st me leave to kisse;
Thou gav'st me leave to wooe;
Thou mad'st me thinke by this,
And that, thou lov'dst me too.

But I shall ne'r forget,
How for to make thee merry;
Thou mad'st me chop, but yet,
Another snapt the Cherry.

Pray and prosper

First offer Incense, then thy field and meads
Shall smile and smell the better by thy beads.
The spangling Dew dreg'd o're the grasse shall be
Turn'd all to Mell, and Manna there for thee.

A Panegerick to Sir Lewis Pemberton

Till I shall come again, let this suffice,
    I send my salt, my sacrifice
To Thee, thy Lady, younglings, and as farre
    As to thy *Genius* and thy *Larre*;
To the worn Threshold, Porch, Hall, Parlour, Kitchin,
    The fat-fed smoking Temple, which in
The wholsome savour of thy mighty Chines
    Invites to supper him who dines,

Where laden spits, warp't with large Ribbs of Beefe,
   Not represent, but give reliefe
To the lanke-Stranger, and the sowre Swain;
   Where both may feed, and come againe:
For no black-bearded *Vigil* from thy doore
   Beats with a button'd-staffe the poore:
But from thy warm-love-hatching gates each may
   Take friendly morsels, and there stay
To Sun his thin-clad members, if he likes,
   For thou no Porter keep'st who strikes.
No commer to thy Roofe his *Guest-rite* wants;
   Or staying there, is scourg'd with taunts
Of some rough Groom, who (yirkt with Corns) sayes, Sir
   Y'ave dipt too long i'th' Vinegar;
And with our Broth and bread, and bits; Sir, friend,
   Y'ave farced well, pray make an end;
Two dayes y'ave larded here; a third, yee know,
   Makes guests and fish smell strong; pray go
You to some other chimney, and there take
   Essay of other giblets; make
Merry at anothers hearth; y'are here
   Welcome as thunder to our beere:
Manners knowes distance, and a man unrude
   Wo'd soon recoile, and not intrude
His Stomach to a second Meale. No, no,
   Thy house, well fed and taught, can show
No such crab'd vizard: Thou hast learnt thy Train,
   With heart and hand to entertain:
And by the Armes-full (with a Brest unhid)*
   As the old Race of mankind did,

   * Brest unhid = open-hearted.

When eithers heart, and eithers hand did strive
      To be the nearer Relative:
Thou do'st redeeme those times; and what was lost
      Of antient honesty, may boast
It keeps a growth in thee; and so will runne
      A course in thy Fames-pledge, *thy Sonne*.
Thus, like a *Roman Tribune*, thou thy gate
      Early setts ope to feast, and late:
Keeping no *currish Waiter* to affright,
      With blasting eye, the appetite,
Which fain would waste upon thy Cates, but that
      The *Trencher-creature* marketh what
Best and more suppling piece he cuts, and by
      Some private pinch tels danger's nie
A hand too desp'rate, or a knife that bites
      Skin deepe into the Porke, or lights
Upon some part of Kid, as if mistooke,
      When checked by the Butlers look.
No, no, thy bread, thy wine, thy jocund Beere
      Is not reserv'd for *Trebius* here,
But all, who at thy table seated are,
      Find equall freedome, equall fare;
And Thou, like to that *Hospitable God*,
      Jove, joy'st when guests make their abode
To eate thy Bullocks thighs, thy Veales, thy fat
      Weathers, and never grudged at.
The *Phesant, Partridge, Gotwit, Reeve, Ruffe, Raile*,
      The *Cock*, the *Curlew*, and the *quaile*;
These, and thy choicest viands do extend
      Their taste unto the lower end
Of thy glad table: not a dish more known
      To thee, than unto any one:

But as thy meate, so thy *immortall wine*
      Makes the smirk face of each to shine,
And spring fresh *Rose-buds*, while the salt, the wit
      Flowes from the Wine, and graces it:
While Reverence, waiting at the bashfull board,
      Honours my Lady and my Lord.
No scurrile jest; no open Sceane is laid
      Here, for to make the face affraid;
But temp'rate mirth dealt forth, and so discreet-
      ly that it makes the meate more sweet;
And adds perfumes unto the Wine, which thou
      Do'st rather poure forth, than allow
By cruse and measure; thus devoting Wine,
      As the *Canary* Isles were thine:
But with that wisdome, and that method, as
      No One that's there his guilty glasse
Drinks of distemper, or ha's cause to cry
      Repentance to his liberty.
No, thou know'st order, Ethicks, and ha's read
      All Oeconomicks, know'st to lead
A House-dance neatly, and can'st truly show,
      How farre a Figure ought to go,
Forward, or backward, side-ward, and what pace
      Can give, and what retract a grace;
What Gesture, Courtship; Comliness agrees,
      With those thy primitive decrees,
To give subsistance to thy house, and proofe,
      What *Genii* support thy roofe,
Goodnes and *Greatnes*; not the oaken Piles;
      For these, and marbles have their whiles

To last, but not their ever: Vertues Hand
        It is, which builds, 'gainst Fate to stand.
Such is thy house, whose firme foundations trust
        Is more in thee, than in her dust,
Or depth, these last may yeeld, and yearly shrinke,
        When what is strongly built, no chinke
Or yawning rupture can the same devoure,
        But fixt it stands, by her own power,
And well-laid bottome, on the iron and rock,
        Which tryes, and counter-stands the shock,
And *Ramme* of time and by vexation growes
        The stronger: *Vertue dies when foes*
Are wanting to her exercise, but great
        And large she spreads by dust, and sweat.
Safe stand thy Walls, and Thee, and so both will,
        Since neithers height was rais'd by th'ill
Of others; since no Stud, no Stone, no Piece,
        Was rear'd up by the Poore-mans fleece:
No Widowes Tenement was rackt to guild
        Or fret thy Seeling, or to build
A *Sweating-Closset*, to annoint the silke-
        soft-skin, or bath in *Asses milke*:
No *Orphans* pittance, left him serv'd to set
        The Pillars up of *lasting Jet*,
For which their cryes might beate against thine eares,
        Or in the dampe Jet read their Teares.
No *Planke* from *Hallowed* Altar, do's appeale
        To yond' *Star-chamber*, or do's seale
A curse to Thee, or Thine; but all things even
        Make for thy peace, and pace to heaven.

Go on directly so, as just men may
      A thousand times, more sweare, than say,
This is that *Princely Pemberton*, who can
      Teach man to keepe a God in man:
And when wise Poets shall search out to see
      Good men, *They find them all in Thee*.

Upon M. Ben. Johnson.　*Epig*.

After the rare Arch-Poet J O H N S O N dy'd,
The Sock grew loathsome, and the Buskins pride,
Together with the Stages glory stood
Each like a poore and pitied widowhood.
The Cirque prophan'd was; and all postures rackt:
For men did strut, and stride, and stare, not act.
Then temper flew from words; and men did squeake,
Looke red, and blow, and bluster, but not speake:
No Holy-Rage, or frantick-fires did stirre,
Or flash about the spacious Theater.
No clap of hands, or shout, or praises-proofe
Did crack the Play-house sides, or cleave her roofe.
Artlesse the Sceane was; and that monstrous sin
Of deep and *arrant ignorance* came in;
Such ignorance as theirs was, who once hist
At thy unequal'd Play, the *Alchymist*:
Oh fie upon 'em! Lastly too, all witt
In utter darkenes did, and still will sit
Sleeping the lucklesse Age out, till that she
Her Resurrection ha's again with Thee.

To his maid Prew

These *Summer-Birds* did with thy Master stay
The times of warmth; but then they flew away;
Leaving their Poet (being now grown old)
Expos'd to all the comming Winters cold.
But thou *kind Prew* did'st with my Fates abide,
As well the Winters, as the Summers Tide:
For which thy Love, live with thy Master here,
Not two, but all the seasons of the yeare.

How Pansies *or* Hearts-ease *came first*

Frollick Virgins once these were,
Overloving, (living here:)
Being here their ends deny'd
Ranne for Sweet-hearts mad, and dy'd.
Love in pitie of their teares,
And their losse in blooming yeares;
For their restlesse here-spent houres,
Gave them *Hearts-ease* turn'd to Flow'rs.

Larr's *portion, and the* Poets *part*

At my homely Country-seat,
I have there a little wheat;
Which I worke to Meale, and make
Therewithall a *Holy-cake*:
Part of which I give to *Larr*,
Part is my peculiar.

Clothes do but cheat and cousen us

Away with silks, away with Lawn,
Ile have no Sceans, or Curtains drawn:
Give me my Mistresse, as she is,
Drest in her nak't simplicities:
For as my Heart, ene so mine Eye
Is wone with flesh, not *Drapery*.

To Dianeme

Shew me thy feet; shew me thy legs, thy thighes;
Shew me Those *Fleshie Principalities*;
Shew me that Hill (where smiling Love doth sit)
Having a living Fountain under it.
Shew me thy waste; Then let me there withall,
By the *Assention* of thy Lawn, see All.

Upon Electra

When out of bed my Love doth spring,
'Tis but as day a kindling:
But when She's up and fully drest,
'Tis then *broad Day throughout the East*.

To his Booke

Have I not blest Thee? Then go forth; nor fear
Or spice, or fish, or fire, or close-stools here.
But with thy fair Fates leading thee, Go on
With thy most white *Predestination*.
Nor thinke these Ages that do hoarcely sing
The *farting Tanner*, and *familiar King*;
The *dancing Frier*, tatter'd in the bush;
Those monstrous lies of little *Robin Rush*:
Tom Chipperfeild, and pritty-*lisping Ned*,
That doted on a Maide of *Gingerbred*:
The *flying Pilcher*, and the *frisking Dace*,
With all the rabble of *Tim-Trundells* race,
(Bred from the dung-hils, and adulterous rhimes,)
Shall live, and thou not superlast all times?
No, no, thy Stars have destin'd Thee to see
The whole world die, and turn to dust with thee.
He's greedie of his life, who will not fall,
When as a publick ruine bears down All.

The mad Maids song

Good morrow to the Day so fair;
   Good morning Sir to you:
Good morrow to mine own torn hair
   Bedabled with the dew.

Good morning to this Prim-rose too;
　　Good morrow to each maid;
That will with flowers the *Tomb* bestrew,
　　Wherein my Love is laid.

Ah woe is me, woe, woe is me,
　　Alack and welladay!
For pitty, Sir, find out that Bee,
　　Which bore my Love away.

Upon the Nipples of Julia's *Breast*

Have ye beheld (with much delight)
A red-Rose peeping through a white?
Or else a Cherrie (double grac't)
Within a Lillie? Center plac't?
Or ever mark't the pretty beam,
A Strawberry shewes halfe drown'd in Creame?
Or seen rich Rubies blushing through
A pure smooth Pearle, and Orient too?
So like to this, nay all the rest,
Is each neate Niplet of her breast.

To Daisies, *not to shut so soone*

Shut not so soon; the dull-ey'd night
　　Ha's not as yet begunne
To make a seisure on the light,
　　Or to seale up the Sun.

No Marigolds yet closed are;
    No shadowes great appeare;
Nor doth the early Shepheards Starre
    Shine like a spangle here.

Stay but till my *Julia* close
    Her life-begetting eye;
And let the whole world then dispose
    It selfe to live or dye.

Oberons *Palace*

After the Feast (my *Shapcot*) see,
The Fairie Court I give to thee:
Where we'le present our *Oberon* led
Halfe tipsie to the Fairie Bed,
Where *Mab* he finds; who there doth lie
Not without mickle majesty.
Which, done; and thence remov'd the light,
We'l wish both Them and Thee, good night.

Full as a Bee with Thyme, and Red,
As Cherry harvest, now high fed
For Lust and action; on he'l go,
To lye with *Mab*, though all say no.
Lust ha's no eares; He's sharpe as thorn;
And fretfull, carries Hay in's horne,*
And lightning in his eyes; and flings
Among the Elves, (if mov'd) the stings

* Hay twisted as a warning round the horns of a dangerous ox.

Of peltish wasps; we'l know his Guard
Kings though th'are hated, will be fear'd.
Wine lead him on. Thus to a Grove
(Sometimes devoted unto Love)
Tinseld with *Twilight*, He, and They
Lead by the shine of Snails; a way
Beat with their num'rous feet, which by
Many a neat perplexity,
Many a turn, and man' a crosse-
Track they redeem* a bank of mosse
Spungie and swelling, and farre more
Soft than the finest Lemster Ore.†
Mildly disparkling, like those fiers,
Which break from the Injeweld tyres
Of curious Brides; or like those mites
Of Candi'd dew in Moony nights.
Upon this *Convex*, all the flowers
(Nature begets by th' Sun, and showers,)
Are to a wilde digestion brought,
As if Loves *Sampler* here was wrought:
Or *Citherea's Ceston*, which
All with temptation doth bewitch.
Sweet Aires move here; and more divine
Made by the breath of great-ey'd kine,
Who as they lowe empearl with milk
The four-leav'd grasse, or mosse-like silk.
The breath of *Munkies* met to mix
With *Musk-flies*, are th' *Aromaticks*,
Which cense this Arch; and here and there,
And farther off, and every where,

* Redeem = reach.   † Leominster wool.

Throughout that *Brave Mosaick* yard
Those Picks or Diamonds in the Card:
With peeps of Harts, of Club and Spade
Are here most neatly inter-laid.
Many a Counter, many a Die,
Half rotten, and without an eye,
Lies here abouts; and for to pave
The excellency of this Cave,
Squirrils and childrens teeth late shed,
Are neatly here enchequered.
With brownest *Toadstones*, and the Gum
That shines upon the blewer Plum.
The nails faln off by Whit-flawes: Art's
Wise hand enchasing here those warts,
Which we to others (from our selves)
Sell, and brought hither by the Elves.
The tempting Mole, stoln from the neck
Of the shie Virgin, seems to deck
The holy Entrance; where within
The roome is hung with the blew skin
Of shifted Snake: enfreez'd throughout
With eyes of Peacocks Trains, and Trout-
flies curious wings; and these among
Those silver-pence, that cut the tongue
Of the red infant, neatly hung.
The glow-wormes eyes; the shining scales
Of silv'rie fish; wheat-strawes, the snailes
Soft Candle-light; the Kitling's eyne;
Corrupted wood; serve here for shine.
No glaring light of bold-fac't Day,
Or other over radiant Ray

Ransacks this roome; but what weak beams
Can make reflected from these jems,
And multiply; Such is the light,
But ever doubtfull Day, or night.
By this quaint Taper-light he winds
His Errours up; and now he finds
His Moon-tann'd *Mab*, as somewhat sick,
And (Love knowes) tender as a chick.
Upon six plump *Dandillions*, high-
Rear'd, lyes her Elvish-majestie:
Whose woollie-bubbles seem'd to drowne
Hir *Mab-ship* in obedient Downe.
For either sheet, was spread the Caule
That doth the Infants face enthrall,
When it is born: (by some enstyl'd
The luckie *Omen* of the child)
And next to these two blankets ore-
Cast of the finest *Gossamore*.
And then a Rug of carded wooll,
Which, *Spunge-like* drinking in the dull-
Light of the Moon, seem'd to comply,
Cloud-like, the *daintie Deitie*.
Thus soft she lies: and over-head
A *Spinners* circle is bespread,
With Cob-web-curtains: from the roof
So neatly sunck, as that no proof
Of any tackling can declare
What gives it hanging in the Aire.
The Fringe about this, are those *Threds*
Broke at the Losse of *Maiden-heads*:

And all behung with these pure Pearls,
Dropt from the eyes of *ravisht Girles*
Or writhing Brides; when, (panting) they
Give unto Love the straiter way.
For Musick now; He has the cries
Of fained-lost-Virginities;
The which the *Elves* make to excite
A more unconquer'd appetite.
The Kings undrest; and now upon
The Gnats-watch-word the *Elves* are gone.
And now the bed, and *Mab* possest
Of this great-little-kingly-Guest.
We'll nobly think, what's to be done,
He'll do no doubt; *This flax is spun.*

To Julia *in the Temple*

Besides us two, i' th' Temple here's not one
To make up now a Congregation.
Let's to the *Altar of perfume* then go,
And say short Prayers; and when we have done so,
Then we shall see, how in a little space,
Saints will come in to fill each Pew and Place.

To Oenone

What Conscience, say, is it in thee
When I a Heart had one,
To Take away that Heart from me,
And to retain thy own?

For shame or pitty now encline
    To play a loving part;
Either to send me kindly thine,
    Or give me back my heart.

Covet not both; but if thou dost
    Resolve to part with neither;
Why! yet to shew that thou art just,
    Take me and mine together.

An Epitaph upon a Virgin

Here a solemne Fast we keepe,
While all beauty lyes asleep
Husht be all things; (no noyse here)
But the toning of a teare:
Or a sigh of such as bring
Cowslips for her covering.

The parting Verse, or charge to his supposed Wife when he travelled

Go hence, and with this parting kisse,
Which joyns two souls, remember this;
Though thou beest young, kind, soft, and faire,
And may'st draw thousands with a haire:
Yet let these glib temptations be
Furies to others, Friends to me.
Looke upon all; and though on fire
Thou set'st their hearts, let chaste desire

Steere Thee to me; and thinke (me gone)
In having all, that thou hast none.
Nor so immured wo'd I have
Thee live, as dead and in thy grave;
But walke abroad, yet wisely well
Stand for my comming, Sentinell.
And think (as thou do'st walke the street)
Me, or my shadow thou do'st meet.
I know a thousand greedy eyes
Will on thy Feature* tirannize,
In my short absence; yet behold
Them like some Picture, or some Mould
Fashion'd like Thee; which though 'tave eares
And eyes, it neither sees or heares.
Gifts will be sent, and Letters, which
Are the expressions of that itch,
And salt, which frets thy Suters; fly
Both, lest thou lose thy liberty:
For that once lost, thou't fall to one,
Then prostrate to a million.
But if they wooe thee, do thou say,
(As that chaste Queen of *Ithaca*
Did to her suitors) this web done
(Undone as oft as done) I'm wonne;
I will not urge Thee, for I know,
Though thou art young, thou canst say no,
And no again, and so deny,
Those thy Lust-burning *Incubi*.
Let them enstile Thee Fairest faire,
The Pearle of Princes, yet despaire

* Feature = Beauty.

That so thou art, because thou must
Believe, Love speaks it not, but Lust;
And this their Flatt'rie do's commend
Thee chiefly for their pleasures end.
I am not jealous of thy Faith,
Or will be; for the Axiome saith,
He that doth suspect, do's haste
A gentle mind to be unchaste.
No, live thee to thy selfe, and keep
Thy thoughts as cold, as is thy sleep:
And let thy dreames be only fed
With this, that I am in thy bed.
And thou then turning in that Sphere,
Waking shalt find me sleeping there.
But yet if boundlesse Lust must skaile
Thy Fortress, and will needs prevaile;
And wildly force a passage in,
Banish consent, and 'tis no sinne
Of Thine; so *Lucrece* fell, and the
Chaste *Syracusian Cyane.*
So *Medullina* fell, yet none
Of these had imputation
For the least trespasse; 'cause the mind
Here was not with the act combin'd.
The body sins not, 'tis the Will
That makes the Action, good, or ill.
And if thy fall sho'd this way come,
Triumph in such a Martirdome.
I will not over-long enlarge
To thee, this my religious charge.
Take this compression, so by this
Means I shall know what other kisse

Is mixt with mine; and truly know,
Returning, if 't be mine or no:
Keepe it till then; and now my Spouse,
For my wisht safety pay thy vowes,
And prayers to *Venus*; if it please
The *Great-blew-ruler* of the Seas;
Not many full-fac't-moons shall waine,
Lean-horn'd, before I come again
As one triumphant; when I find
In thee, all faith of Woman-kind.
Nor wo'd I have thee thinke, that Thou
Had'st power thy selfe to keep this vow;
But having scapt temptations shelfe,
Know vertue taught thee, not thy selfe.

To Blossoms

Faire pledges of a fruitfull Tree,
        Why do yee fall so fast?
        Your date is not so past;
But you may stay yet here a while,
        To blush and gently smile;
        And go at last.

What, were yee borne to be
        An houre or half's delight;
        And so to bid goodnight?
'Twas pitie Nature brought yee forth
        Meerly to shew your worth,
        And lose you quite.

But you are lovely Leaves, where we
    May read how soon things have
      Their end, though ne'r so brave:
And after they have shown their pride,
    Like you a while: They glide
      Into the Grave.

Few fortunate

Many we are, and yet but few possesse
Those Fields of everlasting happinesse.

Upon his departure hence

      Thus I
      Passe by,
      And die:
      As One,
      Unknown,
      And gon:
      I'm made
      A shade,
      And laid
      I'th grave,
      There have
      My Cave.
      Where tell
      I dwell,
      Farewell.

How Springs came first

These Springs were Maidens once that lov'd,
But lost to that they most approv'd:
My Story tells, by Love they were
Turn'd to these Springs, which wee see here:
The pretty whimpering that they make,
When of the Banks their leave they take;
Tels ye but this, they are the same,
In nothing chang'd but in their name.

Upon Julia's *haire fill'd with Dew*

Dew sate on *Julia's* haire,
    And spangled too,
Like Leaves that laden are
    With trembling Dew:
Or glitter'd to my sight,
    As when the Beames
Have their reflected light,
    Daunc't by the Streames.

Upon himselfe

I co'd never love indeed;
Never see mine own heart bleed:
Never crucifie my life;
Or for Widow, Maid, or Wife.

I co'd never seeke to please
One, or many Mistresses:
Never like their lips, to sweare
Oyle of Roses still smelt there.

I co'd never breake my sleepe,
Fold mine Armes, sob, sigh, or weep:
Never beg, or humbly wooe
With oathes, and lyes, (as others do.)

I co'd never walke alone;
Put a shirt of sackcloth on:
Never keep a fast, or pray
For good luck in love (that day.)

But have hitherto liv'd free,
As the aire that circles me:
And kept credit with my heart,
Neither broke i'th whole, or part.

Fresh Cheese and Cream

Wo'd yee have fresh Cheese and Cream?
Julia's Breast can give you them:
And if more; Each *Nipple* cries,
To your *Cream*, her[e]'s *Strawberries*.

An Eclogue, or Pastorall between Endimion
Porter *and* Lycidas Herrick, *set and sung*

Endym. Ah! *Lycidas,* come tell me why
         Thy whilome merry Oate
By thee doth so neglected lye;
         And never purls a Note?

       I prithee speake: *Lyc.* I will *End.* Say on:
Lyc.   'Tis thou, and only thou,
That art the cause *Endimion*;
End.   For Loves-sake, tell me how.

Lyc.   In this regard, that thou do'st play
         Upon an other Plain:
And for a Rurall Roundelay,
         Strik'st now a Courtly strain.

Thou leav'st our Hills, our Dales, our Bowers,
         Our finer fleeced sheep:
(Unkind to us) to spend thine houres,
         Where Shepheards sho'd not keep.

I meane the Court: Let *Latmos* be
         My lov'd *Endymions* Court;
End.   But I the Courtly State wo'd see:
Lyc.   Then see it in report.

What ha's the Court to do with Swaines,
         Where *Phillis* is not known?
Nor do's it mind the Rustick straines
         Of us, or *Coridon.*

Breake, if thou lov'st us, this delay;
End.   Dear *Lycidas*, e're long,
I vow by *Pan*, to come away
    And Pipe unto thy Song.

Then *Jessimine*, with *Florabell*;
    And dainty *Amarillis*,
With handsome-handed *Drosomell*
    Shall pranke thy Hooke with Lillies.

Lyc.   Then *Tityrus*, and *Coridon*,
    And *Thyrsis*, they shall follow
With all the rest; while thou alone
    Shalt lead, like young *Apollo*.

And till thou com'st, thy *Lycidas*,
    In every *Geniall* Cup,
Shall write in Spice, *Endimion* 'twas
    That kept his Piping up.

And my most luckie Swain, when I shall live to see
Endimions Moon to fill up full, remember me:
Mean time, let *Lycidas* have leave to Pipe to thee.

To the *Water Nymphs*, drinking at the *Fountain*

Reach, with your whiter hands, to me,
    Some Christall of the Spring;
And I, about the Cup shall see
    Fresh Lillies flourishing.

Or else sweet Nimphs do you but this;
        To'th' Glasse your lips encline;
And I shall see by that one kisse,
        The Water turn'd to Wine.

Upon himself

Th'art hence removing, (like a Shepherds Tent)
And walk thou must the way that others went:
Fall thou must first, then rise to life with These,
Markt in thy Book for faithfull Witnesses.

On himselfe

Borne I was to meet with Age,
And to walke Life's pilgrimage.
Much I know of Time is spent,
Tell I can't, what's Resident.
Howsoever, cares, adue;
Ile have nought to say to you:
But Ile spend my comming houres,
Drinking wine, and crown'd with flowres.

To Phillis *to love, and live with him*

Live, live with me, and thou shalt see
The pleasures Ile prepare for thee:
What sweets the Country can afford
Shall blesse thy Bed, and blesse thy Board.

The soft sweet Mosse shall be thy bed,
With crawling Woodbine over-spread:
By which the silver-shedding streames
Shall gently melt thee into dreames.
Thy clothing next, shall be a Gowne
Made of the Fleeces purest Downe.
The tongues of Kids shall be thy meate;
Their Milke thy drinke; and thou shalt eate
The Paste of Filberts for thy bread
With Cream of Cowslips buttered:
Thy Feasting-Tables shall be Hills
With *Daisies* spread, and *Daffadils*;
Where thou shalt sit, and *Red-brest* by,
For meat, shall give thee melody.
Ile give thee Chaines and Carkanets
Of *Primroses* and *Violets*.
A Bag and Bottle thou shalt have;
That richly wrought, and This as brave;
So that as either shall expresse
The Wearer's no meane Shepheardesse.
At Sheering-times, and yearely Wakes,
When *Themilis* his pastime makes,
There thou shalt be; and be the wit,
Nay more, the Feast, and grace of it.
On Holy-dayes, when Virgins meet
To dance the Heyes with nimble feet;
Thou shalt come forth, and then appeare
The *Queen of Roses* for that yeere.
And having danc't ('bove all the best)
Carry the Garland from the rest.
In Wicker-baskets Maids shal bring
To thee, (my dearest Shephar[d]ling)

The blushing Apple, bashfull Peare,
And shame-fac't Plum, (all simp'ring there).
Walk in the Groves, and thou shalt find
The name of *Phillis* in the Rind
Of every straight, and smooth-skin tree;
Where kissing that, Ile twice kisse thee.
To thee a Sheep-hook I will send,
Be-pranckt with Ribbands, to this end,
This, this alluring Hook might be
Lesse for to catch a sheep, than me.
Thou shalt have Possets, Wassails fine,
Not made of Ale, but spiced Wine;
To make thy Maids and selfe free mirth,
All sitting neer the glitt'ring Hearth.
Thou sha't have Ribbands, Roses, Rings,
Gloves, Garters, Stockings, Shooes, and Strings
Of winning Colours, that shall move
Others to Lust, but me to Love.
These (nay) and more, thine own shal be,
If thou wilt love, and live with me.

To his Kinswoman, Mistresse Susanna Herrick

When I consider (Dearest) thou dost stay
But here awhile, to languish and decay;
Like to these Garden-glories, which here be
The Flowrie-sweet resemblances of Thee:
With griefe of heart, methinks, I thus doe cry,
Wo'd thou hast ne'r been born, or might'st not die.

Upon her Eyes

Cleere are her eyes,
Like purest Skies.
Discovering from thence
A Babie there
That turns each Sphere,
Like an Intelligence.

Upon her feet

Her pretty feet
Like snailes did creep
A little out, and then,
As if they started at Bo-peep,
Did soon draw in agen.

Upon his gray haires

Fly me not, though I be gray,
Lady, this I know you'l say;
Better look the Roses red,
When with white commingled.
Black your haires are; mine are white;
This begets the more delight,
When things meet most opposite:
As in Pictures we descry,
Venus standing *Vulcan* by.

F

To Electra

'Tis Ev'ning, my Sweet,
And dark; let us meet;
Long time w'ave here been a toying:
And never, as yet,
That season co'd get,
Wherein t'ave had an enjoying.

For pitty or shame,
Then let not Love's flame,
Be ever and ever a spending;
Since now to the Port
The path is but short;
And yet our way has no ending.

Time flyes away fast;
Our houres doe waste:
The while we never remember,
How soone our life, here,
Growes old with the yeere,
That dyes with the next *December*.

To Marygolds

Give way, and be ye ravisht by the Sun,
(And hang the head when as the Act is done)
Spread as He spreads; wax lesse as He do's wane;
And as He shuts, close up to Maids again.

His content in the Country

Here, here I live with what my Board,
Can with the smallest cost afford.
Though ne'r so mean the Viands be,
They well content my *Prew* and me.
Or Pea, or Bean, or Wort, or Beet,
What ever comes, content makes sweet:
Here we rejoyce, because no Rent
We pay for our poore Tenement:
Wherein we rest, and never feare
The Landlord, or the Usurer.
The Quarter-day do's ne'r affright
Our Peacefull slumbers in the night.
We eate our own, and batten more,
Because we feed on no mans score:
But pitie those, whose flanks grow great,
Swel'd with the Lard of others meat.
We blesse our Fortunes, when we see
Our own beloved privacie:
And like our living, where w'are known
To very few, or else to none.

The Fairies

If ye will with *Mab* find grace,
Set each Platter in his place:
Rake the Fier up, and get
Water in, ere Sun be set.

Wash your Pailes, and clense your Dairies;
Sluts are loathsome to the Fairies:
Sweep your house: Who doth not so,
Mab will pinch her by the toe.

The Watch

Man is a Watch, wound up at first, but never
Wound up again: Once down, He's down for ever.
The Watch once downe, all motions then do cease;
And Mans Pulse stopt, *All Passions sleep in Peace.*

Art above Nature, to Julia

When I behold a Forrest spread
With silken trees upon thy head;
And when I see that other Dresse
Of flowers set in comlinesse:
When I behold another grace
In the ascent of curious Lace,
Which like a Pinacle doth shew
The top, and the top-gallant too.
Then, when I see thy Tresses bound
Into an Ovall, square, or round;
And knit in knots far more than I
Can tell by tongue; or true-love tie:
Next, when those Lawnie Filmes I see
Play with a wild civility:

And all those airie silks to flow,
Alluring me, and tempting so:
I must confesse, mine eye and heart
Dotes less on Nature, than on Art.

The Apparition of his Mistresse calling him to Elizium

Desunt nonnulla –

Come then, and like two Doves with silv'rie wings,
Let our soules flie to' th' shades, where ever springs
Sit smiling in the Meads; where Balme and Oile,
Roses and Cassia crown the untill'd soyle.
Where no disease raignes, or infection comes
To blast the Aires, but *Amber-greece* and *Gums*.
This, that, and ev'ry Thicket doth transpire
More sweet, than *Storax* from the hallowed fire:
Where ev'ry tree a wealthy issue beares
Of fragrant Apples, blushing Plums, or Peares:
And all the shrubs, with sparkling spangles, shew
Like Morning-Sun-shine tinsilling the dew.
Here in green Meddowes sits eternall May,
Purfling the Margents, while perpetual Day
So double gilds the Aire, as that no night
Can ever rust th'Enamel of the light.
Here, naked Younglings, handsome Striplings run
Their Goales for Virgins kisses; which when done,
Then unto Dancing forth the learned Round
Commixt they meet, with endlesse Roses crown'd.

And here we'll sit on Primrose-banks, and see
Love's *Chorus* led by *Cupid*; and we'l be
Two loving followers too unto the Grove,
Where Poets sing the stories of our love.
There thou shalt hear Divine *Musæus* sing
Of *Hero*, and *Leander*; then Ile bring
Thee to the Stand, where honour'd *Homer* reades
His *Odisees*, and his high *Iliades*.
About whose Throne the crowd of Poets throng
To heare the incantation of his tongue:
To *Linus*, then to *Pindar*; and that done,
Ile bring thee *Herrick* to *Anacreon*,
Quaffing his full-crown'd bowles of burning Wine,
And in his Raptures speaking Lines of Thine,
Like to His subject; and as his Frantick-
Looks, shew him truly *Bacchanalian* like,
Besmear'd with Grapes; welcome he shall thee thither,
Where both may rage, both drink and dance together.
Then stately *Virgil*, witty *Ovid*, by
Whom faire *Corinna* sits, and doth comply
With Yvorie wrists, his Laureat head, and steeps
His eye in dew of kisses, while he sleeps.
Then soft *Catullus*, sharp-fang'd *Martial*,
And towring *Lucan*, *Horace*, *Juvenal*,
And Snakie *Perseus*, these, and those, whom Rage
(Dropt [from] the jarres of heaven) fill'd t'engage
All times unto their frenzies; Thou shalt there
Behold them in a spacious Theater.
Among which glories, (crown'd with sacred Bayes,
And flatt'ring Ivie) Two recite their Plaies,
Beumont and *Fletcher*, Swans, to whom all eares

Listen, while they (like Syrens in their Spheres)
Sing their *Evadne*; and still more for thee
There yet remaines to know, than thou can'st see
By glim'ring of a fancie: Doe but come,
And there Ile shew thee that capacious roome
In which thye Father *Johnson* now is plac't,
As in a Globe of Radiant fire, and grac't
To be in that Orbe crown'd (that doth include
Those Prophets of the former Magnitude)
And [b]e o[ur] chiefe; But harke, I heare the Cock,
(The Bell-man of the night) proclaime the clock
Of late struck one; and now I see the prime
Of Day break from the pregnant East, 'tis time
I vanish; more I had to say;
But Night determines here, Away.

The Primrose

Aske me why I send you here
This sweet *Infanta* of the yeere?
Aske me why I send to you
This Primrose, thus bepearl'd with dew?
I will whisper to your eares,
The sweets of Love are mixt with tears.

Ask me why this flower do's show
So yellow-green, and sickly too?
Ask me why the stalk is weak
And bending, (yet it doth not break?)
I will answer, These discover
What fainting hopes are in a Lover.

A Frolick

Bring me my Rose-buds, Drawer come;
　　So, while I thus sit crown'd;
Ile drink the aged *Cecubum*,
　　　Untill the roofe turne round.

In the darke none dainty

Night hides our thefts; * all faults then pardon'd be:
All are alike faire, when no spots we see.
Lais and *Lucrece*, in the night time are
Pleasing alike; alike both singular:
Jone, and my *Lady* have at that time one,
One and the selfe-same priz'd complexion.
Then please alike the Pewter and the Plate;
The chosen *Rubie*, and the *Reprobate*.

Upon the troublesome times

　　　O! Times most bad,
　　　Without the scope
　　　　Of hope
　　Of better to be had!

　　　Where shall I goe,
　　　Or whither run
　　　　To shun
　　This publique overthrow?

* Thefts = love affairs.

No places are
(This I am sure)
Secure
In this our wasting Warre.

Some storms w'ave past;
Yet we must all
Down fall,
And perish at the last.

Paines without profit

A long-lifes-day I've taken paines
For very little, or no gaines:
The Ev'ning's come; here now Ile stop,
And work no more; but shut up Shop.

The bad season makes the Poet sad

Dull to my selfe, and almost dead to these
My many fresh and fragrant Mistresses:
Lost to all Musick now; since every thing
Puts on the semblance here of sorrowing.
Sick is the Land to'th' heart; and doth endure
More dangerous faintings by her desp'rate cure.
But if that golden Age wo'd come again,
And *Charles* here Rule, as he before did Raign;
If smooth and unperplext the Seasons were,
As when the *Sweet Maria* lived here:

I sho'd delight to have my Curles halfe drown'd
In *Tyrian Dewes*, and Head with Roses crown'd.
And once more yet (ere I am laid out dead)
Knock at a Starre with my exalted Head.

To the Maids to walke abroad

Come sit we under yonder Tree,
Where merry as the Maids we'l be.
And as on *Primroses* we sit,
We'l venter (if we can) at wit:
If not, at *Draw-gloves* we will play;
So spend some minutes of the day:
Or else spin out the thread of sands,
Playing at *Questions* and *Commands*:
Or tell what strange Tricks Love can do,
By quickly making one of two.
Thus we will sit and talke; but tell
No cruell truths of *Philomell*,
Or *Phyllis*, whom hard Fate forc't on,
To kill her selfe for *Demophon*.
But Fables we'l relate; how *Jove*
Put on all shapes to get a Love:
As now a *Satyr*, then a *Swan*;
A *Bull* but then; and now a man.
Next we will act how young men wooe,
And sigh, and kiss, as Lovers do:
And talke of Brides; and who shall make
That wedding-smock, this Bridal-Cake;

That Dress, this Sprig, that Leaf, this Vine;
That smooth and silken Columbine.
This done, we'l draw lots, who shall buy
And guild the Baies and Rosemary:
What Poses for our Wedding Rings;
What Gloves we'l give, and Ribanings:
And smiling at our selves, decree,
Who then the joyning *Priest* shall be.
What short sweet Prayers shall be said;
And how the Posset shall be made
With Cream of Lillies (not of Kine)
And *Maiden's-blush*, for spiced wine.
Thus, having talkt, we'l next commend
A kiss to each; and *so we'l end.*

The Night-piece, to Julia

Her Eyes the Glow-worme lend thee,
  The Shooting Starres attend thee;
     And the Elves also,
     Whose little eyes glow,
Like the sparks of fire, befriend thee.

  No *Will-o'-th'-Wispe* mis-light thee;
  Nor Snake, or Slow-worme bite thee:
     But on, on thy way
     Not making a stay,
Since Ghost ther's none to affright thee.

Let not the darke thee cumber;
What though the Moon do's slumber?
    The Starres of the night
    Will lend thee their light,
Like Tapers cleare without number.

Then *Julia* let me wooe thee,
Thus, thus to come unto me:
    And when I shall meet
    Thy silv'ry feet,
My soule Ile poure into thee.

His charge to Julia *at his death*

Dearest of thousands, now the time drawes neere,
That with my Lines, my Life must full-stop here.
Cut off thy haires; and let thy Teares be shed
Over my Turfe, when I am buried.
Then for *effusions*, let none wanting be,
Or other Rites that doe belong to me;
As Love shall helpe thee, when thou do'st go hence
Unto thy everlasting residence.

The Coblers Catch

Come sit we by the fires side;
    And roundly drinke we here;
Till that we see our cheekes Ale-dy'd
    And noses tann'd with Beere.

To his lovely Mistresses

One night i' th' yeare, my dearest Beauties, come
And bring those *dew-drink-offerings* to my Tomb.
When thence ye see my reverend Ghost to rise,
And there to lick th' effused sacrifice:
Though palenes be the Livery that I weare,
Looke ye not wan, or colourlesse for feare.
Trust me I will not hurt ye; or once shew
The least grim looke, or cast a frown on you:
Nor shall the Tapers when I'm there, burn blew.
This I may do (perhaps) as I glide by,
Cast on my Girles a glance, and loving eye:
Or fold mine armes, and sigh, because I've lost
The world so soon, and in it, you the most.
Than these, no feares more on your Fancies fall,
Though then I smile, and speake no words at all.

The Beggar to Mab, *the* Fairie Queen

Please your Grace, from out your Store,
Give an Almes to one that's poore,
That your mickle, may have more.
Black I'm grown for want of meat;
Give me then an Ant to eate;
Or the cleft eare of a Mouse
Over-sowr'd in drinke of Souce:
Or *sweet Lady* reach to me
The *Abdomen* of a Bee;

Or commend a *Crickets-hip*,
Or his *Huckson*,* to my Scrip.
Give for bread, a little bit
Of a Pease, that 'gins to chit,
And my full thanks take for it.
Floure of Fuz-balls, that's too good
For a man in needy-hood:
But the Meal of Mill-dust can
Well content a craving man.
Any Orts the Elves refuse
Well will serve the Beggars use.
But if this may seem too much
For an Almes; then give me such
Little bits, that nestle there
In the Pris'ners *Panier*.
So a blessing light upon
You, and mighty *Oberon*:
That your plenty last till when,
I return your Almes agen.

The Hag

The Hag is astride,
This night for to ride;
The Devill and shee together:
Through thick, and through thin,
Now out, and then in,
Though ne'r so foule be the weather.

---

* *Huckson* (Hockshin) = underside of the thigh.

A Thorn or a Burr
She takes for a Spurre:
With a lash of a Bramble she rides now,
Through Brakes and through Bryars,
O're Ditches, and Mires,
She followes the Spirit that guides now.

No Beast, for his food,
Dares now range the wood;
But husht in his laire he lies lurking:
While mischeifs, by these,
On Land and on Seas,
At noone of Night are a working.

The storme will arise,
And trouble the skies;
This night, and more for the wonder,
The ghost from the Tomb
Affrighted shall come,
Cal'd out by the clap of the Thunder.

To his Closet-Gods

When I goe Hence ye *Closet-Gods*, I feare
Never againe to have ingression here:
Where I have had, what ever thing co'd be
Pleasant, and precious to my Muse and me.
Besides rare sweets, I had a Book which none
Co'd reade the Intext but my selfe alone.
About the Cover of this Book there went
A curious-comely clean *Compart[i]ement*:

And, in the midst, to grace it more, was set
A blushing-pretty-peeping Rubelet:
But now 'tis clos'd; and being shut, and seal'd,
Be it, O be it, never more reveal'd!
Keep here still, *Closet-Gods*, 'fore whom I've set
Oblations oft, of sweetest Marmelet.

The Country life, to the honoured M. End. Porter, *Groome of the Bed-Chamber to his Maj*.

Sweet Country life, to such unknown,
Whose lives are others, not their own!
But serving Courts, and Cities, be
Less happy, less enjoying thee.
Thou never Plow'st the Oceans foame
To seek, and bring rough Pepper home:
Nor to the Eastern Ind dost rove
To bring from thence the scorched Clove.
Nor, with the losse of thy lov'd rest,
Bring'st home the Ingot from the West.
No, thy Ambition's Master-piece
Flies no thought higher than a fleece:
Or how to pay thy Hinds, and cleere
All scores; and so to end the yeere:
But walk'st about thine own dear bounds,
Not envying others larger grounds:
For well thou know'st, *'tis not th' extent*
Of Land makes life, but sweet content.
When now the Cock (the Plow-mans Horne)
Calls forth the lilly-wristed Morne;

Then to thy corn-fields thou dost goe,
Which though well soyl'd, yet thou dost know,
That the best compost for the Lands
Is the wise Masters Feet, and Hands.
There at the Plough thou find'st thy Teame,
With a Hind whistling there to them:
And cheer'st them up, by singing how
The Kingdoms portion *is the Plow*.
This done, then to th' enameld Meads
Thou go'st; and as thy foot there treads,
Thou seest a present God-like Power
Imprinted in each Herbe and Flower:
And smell'st the breath of great-ey'd Kine,
Sweet as the blossomes of the Vine.
Here thou behold'st thy large sleek Neat
Unto the Dew-laps up in meat:
And, as thou look'st, the wanton Steere,
The Heifer, Cow, and Oxe draw neere
To make a pleasing pastime there.
These seen, thou go'st to view thy flocks
Of sheep, (safe from the Wolfe and Fox)
And find'st their bellies there as full
Of short sweet grasse, as backs with wool.
And leav'st them (as they feed and fill)
A Shepherd piping on a hill.
For Sports, for Pagentrie, and Playes,
Thou hast thy Eves, and Holydayes:
On which the young men and maids meet,
To exercise their dancing feet:
Tripping the comely country round,
With Daffadils and Daisies crown'd.

Thy Wakes, thy Quintels, here thou hast,
Thy May-poles too with Garlands grac't:
Thy Morris-dance; thy Whitsun-ale;
Thy Sheering-feast, which never faile.
Thy Harvest home; thy Wassaile bowle,
That's tost up after Fox i' th' Hole.
Thy Mummeries; thy Twelfe-tide Kings
And Queenes; thy Christmas revellings:
Thy Nut-browne mirth; thy Russet wit;
And no man payes too deare for it.
To these, thou hast thy times to goe
And trace the Hare i' th' trecherous Snow:
Thy witty wiles to draw, and get
The Larke into the Trammell net:
Thou hast thy Cockrood, and thy Glade
To take the precious Phesant made:
Thy Lime-twigs, Snares, and Pit-falls then
To catch the pilfring Birds, not Men.
O happy life! if that their good
The Husbandmen but understood!
Who all the day themselves doe please,
And Younglings, with such sports as these.
And, lying down, have nought t' affright
Sweet sleep, that makes more short the night.

Cætera desunt —

To Electra

I dare not ask a kisse;
    I dare not beg a smile;
Lest having that, or this,
    I might grow proud the while.

No, no, the utmost share
    Of my desire, shall be
Onely to kisse that Aire,
    That lately kissed thee.

What kind of Mistresse he would have

Be the Mistresse of my choice,
Cleane in manners, cleere in voice:
Be she witty, more than wise;
Pure enough, though not Precise:
Be she shewing in her dresse,
Like a civill Wilderness;
That the curious may detect
Order in a sweet neglect:
Be she rowling in her eye,
Tempting all the passers by:
And each Ringlet of her haire,
An Enchantment, or a Snare,
For to catch the Lookers on;
But her self held fast by none.
Let her *Lucrece* all day be,
Thais in the night, to me.
Be she such, as neither will
Famish me, nor over-fill.

Once seen, and no more

Thousands each day passe by, which wee,
Once past and gone, no more shall see.

To Fortune

Tumble me down, and I will sit
Upon my ruines (smiling yet:)
Teare me to tatters; yet I'le be
Patient in my necessitie.
Laugh at my scraps of cloaths, and shun
Me, as a fear'd infection:
Yet scarre-crow-like I'le walk, as one,
Neglecting thy derision.

Stool-ball

At Stool-ball, *Lucia*, let us play,
    For Sugar-cakes and Wine;
Or for a Tansie* let us pay,
    The losse or thine, or mine.

If thou, my Deere, a winner be
    At trundling of the Ball,
The wager thou shalt have, and me,
    And my misfortunes all.

But if (my Sweetest) I shall get,
    Then I desire but this;
That likewise I may pay the Bet,
    And have for all a kisse.

* Tansie = a dish flavoured with tansy.

The Bracelet of Pearle: to Silvia

I brake thy Bracelet 'gainst my will;
 And, wretched, I did see
Thee discomposed then, and still
 Art discontent with me.

One jemme was lost; and I will get
 A richer pearle for thee,
Than ever, dearest *Silvia*, yet
 Was drunk to *Antonie*.

Or, for revenge, I'le tell thee what
 Thou for the breach shalt do;
First, crack the strings, and after that,
 Cleave thou my heart in two.

Teares, and Laughter

Knew'st thou, one moneth wo'd take thy life away,
Thou'dst weep; but laugh, sho'd it not last a day.

His returne to London

From the dull confines of the drooping West,
To see the day spring from the pregnant East,
Ravisht in spirit, I come, nay more, I flie
To thee, blest place of my Nativitie!
Thus, thus with hallowed foot I touch the ground,
With thousand blessings by thy Fortune crown'd.

O fruitfull Genius! that bestowest here
An everlasting plenty, yeere by yeere.
O *Place*! O *People*! Manners! fram'd to please
All *Nations, Customes, Kindreds, Languages*!
I am a free-born *Roman*; suffer then,
That I amongst you live a Citizen.
London my home is: though by hard fate sent
Into a long and irksome banishment;
Yet since cal'd back; henceforward let me be,
O native countrey, repossest by thee!
For, rather than I'le to the West return,
I'le beg of thee first here to have mine Urn.
Weak I am grown, and must in short time fall;
Give thou my sacred Reliques Buriall.

His Grange, or private wealth

Though Clock,
To tell how night drawes hence, I've none,
A Cock,
I have, to sing how day drawes on.
I have
A maid (my *Prew*) by good luck sent,
To save
That little, Fates me gave or lent.
A Hen
I keep, which creeking day by day,
Tells when
She goes her long white egg to lay.

A Goose
I have, which, with a jealous eare,
Lets loose
Her tongue, to tell what danger's neare.
A Lamb
I keep (tame) with my morsells fed,
Whose Dam
An Orphan left him (lately dead.)
A Cat
I keep, that playes about my House,
Grown fat,
With eating many a miching Mouse.
To these
A *Trasy** I do keep, whereby
I please
The more my rurall privacie:
Which are
But toyes, to give my heart some ease:
Where care
None is, slight things do lightly please.

Upon Lucia *dabled in the deaw*

My *Lucia* in the deaw did go,
And prettily bedabled so,
Her cloaths held up, she shew'd withall
Her decent legs, cleane, long and small.

* His Spaniel.

I follow'd after to descrie
Part of the nak't sincerity;
But still the envious Scene between
Deni'd the Mask I wo'd have seen.

A Ternarie of littles, upon a pipkin of
Jellie sent to a Lady

A little Saint best fits a little Shrine,
A little prop best fits a little Vine,
As my small Cruse best fits my little Wine.

A little Seed best fits a little Soyle,
A little Trade best fits a little Toyle:
As my small Jarre best fits my little Oyle.

A little Bin best fits a little Bread,
A little Garland fits a little Head:
As my small stuffe best fits my little Shed.

A little Hearth best fits a little Fire,
A little Chappell fits a little Quire,
As my small Bell best fits my little Spire.

A little streame best fits a little Boat;
A little lead best fits a little Float;
As my small Pipe best fits my little note.

A little meat best fits a little bellie,
As sweetly Lady, give me leave to tell ye,
This little Pipkin fits this little Jellie.

Lovers how they come and part

A *Gyges* Ring they beare about them still,
To be, and not seen when and where they will.
They tread on clouds, and though they sometimes fall,
They fall like dew, but make no noise at all.
So silently they one to th' other come,
As colours steale into the Peare or Plum,
And Aire-like, leave no pression to be seen
Where e're they met, or parting place has been.

The Apron of Flowers

To gather Flowers *Sappha* went,
    And homeward she did bring
Within her Lawnie Continent,
    The treasure of the Spring.

She smiling blusht, and blushing smil'd,
    And sweetly blushing thus,
She lookt as she'd been got with child
    By young *Favonius*.

Her Apron gave (as she did passe)
    An Odor more divine,
More pleasing too, than ever was
    The lap of *Proserpine*.

Love dislikes nothing

Whatsoever thing I see,
Rich or poore although it be;
'Tis a Mistresse unto mee.

Be my Girle, or faire or browne,
Do's she smile, or do's she frowne:
Still I write a Sweet-heart downe.

Be she rough, or smooth of skin;
When I touch, I then begin
For to let Affection in.

Be she bald, or do's she weare
Locks incurl'd of other haire;
I shall find enchantment there.

Be she whole, or be she rent,
So my fancie be content,
She's to me most excellent.

Be she fat, or be she leane,
Be she sluttish, be she cleane,
I'm a man for ev'ry Sceane.

The Wake

Come *Anthea* let us two
Go to Feast, as others do.
Tarts and Custards, Creams and Cakes,
Are the Junketts still at Wakes:

Unto which the Tribes resort,
Where the businesse is the sport:
Morris-dancers thou shalt see,
Marian too in Pagentrie:
And a Mimick to devise
Many grinning properties.
Players there will be, and those
Base in action as in clothes:
Yet with strutting they will please
The incurious Villages.
Neer the dying of the day,
There will be a *Cudgell*-Play,
Where a *Coxcomb* will be broke,
Ere a good *word* can be spoke:
But the anger ends all here,
Drencht in Ale, or drown'd in Beere.
Happy Rusticks, best content
With the cheapest Merriment:
And possesse no other feare,
Than to want the Wake next Yeare.

To Doctor Alablaster

Nor art thou lesse esteem'd, that I have plac'd
(Amongst mine honour'd) Thee (almost) the last:
In great Processions many lead the way
To him, who is the triumph of the day,
As these have done to Thee, who art the one,
One onely glory of a million,

In whom the spirit of the Gods do's dwell,
Firing thy soule, by which thou dost foretell
When this or that vast *Dinastie* must fall
Downe to a *Fillit* more *Imperiall*.
When this or that *Horne* shall be broke, and when
Others shall spring up in their place agen:
When times and seasons and all yeares must lie
Drown'd in the Sea of wild Eternitie:
When the *Black Dooms-day Bookes* (as yet unseal'd)
Shall by the mighty *Angell* be reveal'd:
And when the Trumpet which thou late hast found
Shall call to Judgment; tell us when the sound
Of this or that great Aprill day shall be,
And next the Gospell wee will credit thee.
Meane time like Earth-wormes we will craule below,
And wonder at Those Things that thou dost know.

A Conjuration, to Electra

By those soft Tods of wooll
With which the aire is full:
By all those Tinctures there,
That paint the *Hemisphere*:
By Dewes and drisling Raine,
That swell the Golden Graine:
By all those sweets that be
I'th flowrie Nunnerie:
By silent Nights, and the
Three Formes of *Heccate*:

By all Aspects that blesse
The sober *Sorceresse*,
While juice she straines, and pith
To make her Philters with:
By Time, that hastens on
Things to perfection:
And by your self, the best
Conjurement of the rest:
O my *Electra*! be
In love with none, but me.

The Spell

Holy Water come and bring;
Cast in Salt, for seasoning:
Set the Brush for sprinkling:
Sacred Spittle bring ye hither;
Meale and it now mix together;
And a little Oyle to either:
Give the Tapers here their light,
Ring the *Saints-Bell*, to affright
Far from hence the evill Sp'rite.

A Hymne to Bacchus

I sing thy praise *Iacchus*,
Who with thy *Thyrse* dost thwack us:
And yet thou so dost back us
With boldness that we feare
No *Brutus* entring here;
Nor *Cato* the severe.
What though the *Lictors* threat us,
We know they dare not beate us;
So long as thou dost heat us.
When we thy *Orgies* sing,
Each Cobler is a King;
Nor dreads he any thing:
And though he doe not rave,
Yet he'l the courage have
To call my *Lord Maior* knave;
Besides too, in a brave,
Although he has no riches,
But walks with dangling breeches,
And skirts that want their stiches,
And shewes his naked flitches;
Yet he'le be thought or seen,
So good as *George-a-Green*;
And calls his Blouze, his Queene;
And speaks in language keene:
O *Bacchus*! let us be
From cares and troubles free;
And thou shalt heare how we
Will chant new *Hymnes* to thee.

Upon Julia's *Clothes*

When as in silks my *Julia* goes,
Then, then (me thinks) how sweetly flowes
That liquefaction of her clothes.

Next, when I cast mine eyes and see
That brave Vibration each way free;
O how that glittering taketh me!

Upon Prew *his Maid*

In this little Urne is laid
Prewdence Baldwin (once my maid)
From whose happy spark here let
Spring the purple Violet.

The Maiden-blush

So look the mornings when the Sun
Paints them with fresh Vermilion:
So Cherries blush, and Kathern Peares,
And Apricocks, in youthfull yeares:
So Corrolls looke more lovely Red,
And Rubies lately polished:
So purest Diaper doth shine,
Stain'd by the Beames of Clarret wine:
As *Julia* looks when she doth dress
Her either cheeke with bashfullness.

To my dearest Sister M. Mercie Herrick

When ere I go, or what so ere befalls
Me in mine Age, or forraign Funerals,
This Blessing I will leave thee, ere I go,
Prosper thy Basket, and therein thy Dow.
Feed on the paste of Filberts, or else knead
And Bake the floure of Amber for thy bread.
Balm may thy Trees drop, and thy Springs runne oyle
And everlasting Harvest crown thy Soile!
These I but wish for; but thy selfe shall see,
The Blessing fall in mellow times on Thee.

To Julia, *in her Dawn, or Day-breake*

By the next kindling of the day
        My *Julia* thou shalt see,
Ere *Ave-Mary* thou canst say
        Ile come and visit thee.

Yet ere thou counsel'st with thy Glasse,
        Appeare thou to mine eyes
As smooth, and nak't, as she that was
        The prime of *Paradice.*

If blush thou must, then blush thou through
        A Lawn, that thou mayst looke
As purest Pearles, or Pebles do
        When peeping through a Brooke.

As Lillies shrin'd in Christall, so
    Do thou to me appeare;
Or Damask Roses, when they grow
    To sweet acquaintance there.

Upon Love

Love brought me to a silent Grove,
    And shew'd me there a Tree,
Where some had hang'd themselves for love,
    And gave a Twist to me.

The Halter was of silk, and gold,
    That he reacht forth unto me:
No otherwise, than if he would
    By dainty things undo me.

He bade me then that Neck-lace use;
    And told me too, he maketh
A glorious end by such a Noose,
    His Death for Love that taketh.

'Twas but a dream; but had I been
    There really alone;
My desp'rate feares, in love, had seen
    Mine Execution.

G

Kisses Loathsome

I abhor the slimie kisse,
(Which to me most loathsome is.)
Those lips please me which are plac't
Close, but not too strictly lac't:
Yeilding I wo'd have them; yet
Not a wimbling* Tongue admit:
What sho'd poking-sticks† make there,
When the ruffe is set elsewhere?

Upon Julia's *haire, bundled up in a golden net*

Tell me, what needs those rich deceits,
These golden Toyles, and Trammel-nets,
To take thine haires when they are knowne
Already tame, and all thine owne?
'Tis I am wild, and more than haires
Deserve these Mashes and those snares.
Set free thy Tresses, let them flow
As aires doe breathe, or winds doe blow:
And let such curious Net-works be
Lesse set for them, than spred for me.

    * Wimbling = boring a hole.
    † Poking-sticks, for stiffening ruffs.

Ceremonies for Candlemasse Eve

Down with the Rosemary and Bayes,
　　Down with the Misleto;
In stead of Holly, now up-raise
　　The greener Box (for show.)

The Holly hitherto did sway;
　　Let Box now domineere;
Untill the dancing Easter-day,
　　Or Easters Eve appeare.

Then youthfull Box which now hath grace,
　　Your houses to renew;
Grown old, surrender must his place,
　　Unto the crisped Yew.

When Yew is out, then Birch comes in,
　　And many Flowers beside;
Both of a fresh, and fragrant kinne
　　To honour Whitsontide.

Green Rushes then, and sweetest Bents,
　　With cooler Oken boughs;
Come in for comely ornaments,
　　To re-adorn the house.
Thus times do shift; each thing his turne do's hold;
New things succeed, as former things grow old.

The Ceremonies for Candlemasse day

Kindle the Christmas Brand, and then
    Till Sunne-set, let it burne;
Which quencht, then lay it up agen,
    Till Christmas next returne.
Part must be kept wherewith to teend
    The Christmas Log next yeare;
And where 'tis safely kept, the Fiend,
    Can do no mischiefe (there.)

To his Book

Before the Press scarce one co'd see
A little-peeping-part of thee:
But since th'art Printed, thou dost call
To shew thy nakedness to all.
My care for thee is now the less;
(Having resign'd thy shamefac'tness:)
Go with thy Faults and Fates; yet stay
And take this sentence, then away;
Whom one belov'd will not suffice,
She'l runne to all adulteries.

Upon Ben. Johnson

Here lyes *Johnson* with the rest
Of the Poets; but the Best.

Reader, wo'dst thou more have known?
Aske his Story, not this Stone.
That will speake what this can't tell
Of his glory. *So farewell.*

An Ode for him

Ah *Ben*!
Say how, or when
Shall we thy Guests
Meet at those *Lyrick* Feasts,
Made at the *Sun*,
The *Dog*, the triple *Tunne*?
Where we such clusters had,
As made us nobly wild, not mad;
And yet each Verse of thine
Out-did the meate, out-did the frolick wine.

My *Ben*
Or come agen:
Or send to us,
Thy wits great over-plus;
But teach us yet
Wisely to husband it;
Lest we that Tallent spend:
And having once brought to an end
That precious stock; the store
Of such a wit the world sho'd have no more.

Revenge

Mans disposition is for to requite
An injurie, before a benefite:
Thanksgiving is a burden, and a paine;
Revenge is pleasing to us, as our gaine.

The present time best pleaseth

Praise they that will Times past, I joy to see
My selfe now live: *this age best pleaseth mee.*

Upon Julia's *washing her self in the river*

How fierce was I, when I did see
My *Julia* wash her self in thee!
So *Lillies* thorough Christall look:
So purest pebbles in the brook:
As in the River *Julia* did,
Halfe with a Lawne of water hid,
Into thy streames my self I threw,
And strugling there, I kist thee too;
And more had done (it is confest)
Had not thy waves forbad the rest.

Upon Clunn

A rowle of Parchment *Clunn* about him beares,
Charg'd with the Armes of all his Ancestors:
And seems halfe ravisht, when he looks upon
That *Bar*, this *Bend*; that *Fess*, this *Cheveron*;
This *Manch*, that *Moone*; this *Martlet*, and that
  Mound;
This counterchange of *Perle* and *Diamond*.
What joy can *Clun* have in that Coat, or this,
When as his owne still out at elboes is?

Leven

Love is a Leven, and a loving kisse
The Leven of a loving sweet-heart is.

Ceremony upon Candlemas Eve

Down with the Rosemary, and so
Down with the Baies, and misletoe:
Down with the Holly, Ivie, all,
Wherewith ye drest the Christmas Hall:
That so the superstitious find
No one least Branch there left behind:
For look how many leaves there be
Neglected there (maids trust to me)
So many *Goblins* you shall see.

Anacreontike

I must
Not trust
Here to any;
Bereav'd,
Deceiv'd
By so many:
As one
Undone
By my losses;
Comply
Will I
With my crosses.
Yet still
I will
Not be grieving;
Since thence
And hence
Comes relieving.
But this
Sweet is
In our mourning;
Times bad
And sad
Are a turning:
And he
Whom we
See dejected;
Next day
Wee may
See erected.

His Grange

How well contented in this private *Grange*
Spend I my life (that's subject unto change:)
Under whose Roofe with *Mosse-worke* wrought, there I
Kisse my *Brown wife*, and *black Posterity*.

Leprosie in Cloathes

When flowing garments I behold
Enspir'd with *Purple*, *Pearle*, and *Gold*;
I think no other but I see
In them a glorious leprosie
That do's infect, and make the rent
More mortall in the vestiment.
As flowrie vestures doe descrie
The wearers rich immodestie;
So plaine and simple cloathes doe show
Where vertue walkes, not those that flow.

The Vision

Me thought I saw (as I did dreame in bed)
A crawling Vine about *Anacreon's* head:
Flusht was his face; his haires with oyle did shine;
And as he spake, his mouth ranne ore with wine.
Tipled he was; and tipling lispt withall;
And lisping reeld, and reeling like to fall.
A young *Enchantresse* close by him did stand
Tapping his plump thighes with a *mirtle* wand:
She smil'd; he kist; and kissing, cull'd her too;
And being cup-shot, more he co'd not doe.
For which (me thought) in prittie anger she
Snatcht off his Crown, and gave the wreath to me:
Since when (me thinks) my braines about doe swim,
And I am wilde and wanton like to him.

Comfort to a youth that had lost his Love

What needs complaints,
When she a place
Has with the race
        Of Saints?
In endlesse mirth,
She thinks not on
What's said or done
        In earth:
She sees no teares,
Or any tone
Of thy deep grone
        She heares:

Nor do's she minde,
Or think on't now,
That ever thou
Wast kind.
But chang'd above,
She likes not there,
As she did here,
Thy Love.
Forbeare therefore,
And Lull asleepe
Thy woes and weep
No more.

His teares to Thamasis

I send, I send here my supremest kiss
To thee my *silver-footed Thamasis.*
No more shall I reiterate thy Strand,
Whereon so many Stately Structures stand:
Nor in the summers sweeter evenings go,
To bath in thee (as thousand others doe.)
No more shall I a long thy christall glide,
In Barge (with boughes and rushes beautifi'd)
With soft-smooth Virgins (for our chast disport)
To *Richmond, Kingstone,* and to *Hampton-Court*:
Never againe shall I with Finnie-Ore
Put from, or draw unto the faithfull shore:
And Landing here, or safely Landing there,
Make way to my *Beloved Westminster*:

Or to the *Golden-cheap-side*, where the earth
Of *Julia Herrick* gave to me my Birth.
May all clean *Nimphs* and curious water Dames,
With Swan-like-state, flote up and down thy streams:
No drought upon thy wanton waters fall
To make them Leane, and languishing at all.
No ruffling winds come hither to discease
Thy pure, and *Silver-wristed Naides*.
Keep up your state ye streams; and as ye spring,
Never make sick your Banks by surfeiting.
Grow young with Tydes, and though I see ye never,
Receive this vow, *so fare-ye-well for ever*.

His desire

Give me a man that is not dull,
When all the world with rifts is full:
But unamaz'd dares clearely sing,
When as the roof's a tottering:
And, though it falls, continues still
Tickling the *Citterne* with his quill.

To his Girles who would have him sportfull

Alas I can't, for tell me how
Can I be gamesome (aged now)
Besides ye see me daily grow
Here Winter-like, to Frost and Snow.
And I ere long, my Girles, shall see,
Ye quake for cold to looke on me.

To his Brother Nicolas Herrick

What others have with cheapnesse seene, and ease,
In Varnisht maps; by'th' helpe of Compasses:
Or reade in Volumes, and those Bookes (with all
Their large Narrations, *Incanonicall*)
Thou hast beheld those seas, and Countries farre;
And tel'st to us, what once they were, and are.
So that with bold truth, thou canst now relate
This Kingdomes fortune, and that Empires fate:
Canst talke to us of *Sharon*; where a spring
Of Roses have an endlesse flourishing.
Of *Sion*, *Sinai*, *Nebo*, and with them,
Make knowne to us the now *Jerusalem*.
The Mount of *Olives*; *Calverie*, and where
Is (and hast seene) *thy Saviours Sepulcher*.
So that the man that will but lay his eares,
As *Inapostate*, to the thing he heares,
Shall by his hearing quickly come to see
The truth of Travails lesse in bookes than Thee.

The mount of the Muses

After thy labour take thine ease,
Here with the sweet *Pierides*.
But if so be that men will not
Give thee the Laurell Crowne for lot;
Be yet assur'd, thou shalt have one
Not subject to corruption.

To his Book's end this last line he'd have plac't,
Jocond his Muse was; but his Life was chast.

* *

*

FROM

Noble Numbers

Upon Time

Time was upon
The wing, to flie away;
And I cal'd on
Him but a while to stay;
But he'd be gone,
For ought that I could say.

He held out then,
A Writing, as he went;
And askt me, when
False man would be content
To pay agen,
What God and Nature lent.

An houre-glasse,
In which were sands but few,
As he did passe,
He shew'd, and told me too,
Mine end near was,
And so away he flew.

His Letanie, to the Holy Spirit

In the houre of my distresse,
When temptations me oppresse,
And when I my sins confesse,
      Sweet Spirit comfort me!

When I lie within my bed,
Sick in heart, and sick in head,
And with doubts discomforted,
     Sweet Spirit comfort me!

When the house doth sigh and weep,
And the world is drown'd in sleep,
Yet mine eyes the watch do keep;
     Sweet Spirit comfort me!

When the artlesse Doctor sees
No one hope, but of his Fees,
And his skill runs on the lees;
     Sweet Spirit comfort me!

When his Potion and his Pill,
His, or none, or little skill,
Meet for nothing, but to kill;
     Sweet Spirit comfort me!

When the passing-bell doth tole,
And the Furies in a shole
Come to fright a parting soule;
     Sweet Spirit comfort me!

When the tapers now burne blew,
And the comforters are few,
And that numbers more than true;
     Sweet Spirit comfort me!

When the Priest his last hath praid,
And I nod to what is said,
'Cause my speech is now decaid;
     Sweet Spirit comfort me!

When (God knowes) I'm tost about,
Either with despaire, or doubt;
Yet before the glasse be out,
  Sweet Spirit comfort me!

When the Tempter me pursu'th
With the sins of all my youth,
And halfe damns me with untruth;
  Sweet Spirit comfort me!

When the flames and hellish cries
Fright mine eares, and fright mine eyes,
And all terrors me surprize;
  Sweet Spirit comfort me!

When the Judgment is reveal'd,
And that open'd which was seal'd,
When to Thee I have appeal'd;
  Sweet Spirit comfort me!

A Thanksgiving to God, for his House

Lord, Thou hast given me a cell
  Wherein to dwell;
And little house, whose humble Roof
  Is weather-proof;
Under the sparres of which I lie
  Both soft, and drie;
Where Thou my chamber for to ward
  Hast set a Guard

Of harmlesse thoughts, to watch and keep
       Me, while I sleep.
Low is my porch, as is my Fate,
       Both void of state;
And yet the threshold of my doore
       Is worn by'th poore,
Who thither come, and freely get
       Good words, or meat:
Like as my Parlour, so my Hall
       And Kitchin's small:
A little Butterie, and therein
       A little Byn,
Which keeps my little loafe of Bread
       Unchipt, unflead:
Some brittle sticks of Thorne or Briar
       Make me a fire,
Close by whose living coale I sit,
       And glow like it.
Lord, I confesse too, when I dine,
       The Pulse is Thine,
And all those other Bits, that bee
       There plac'd by Thee;
The Worts, the Purslain, and the Messe
       Of Water-cresse,
Which of Thy kindnesse Thou hast sent;
       And my content
Makes those, and my beloved Beet,
       To be more sweet.
'Tis Thou that crown'st my glittering Hearth
       With guiltlesse mirth;

And giv'st me Wassaile Bowles to drink,
　　　Spic'd to the brink.
Lord, 'tis thy plenty-dropping hand,
　　　That soiles my land;
And giv'st me, for my Bushell sowne,
　　　Twice ten for one:
Thou mak'st my teeming Hen to lay
　　　Her egg each day:
Besides my healthfull Ewes to beare
　　　Me twins each yeare:
The while the conduits of my Kine
　　　Run Creame, (for Wine.)
All these, and better Thou dost send
　　　Me, to this end,
That I should render, for my part,
　　　A thankfull heart;
Which, fir'd with incense, I resigne,
　　　As wholly Thine;
But the acceptance, that must be,
　　　My Christ, by Thee.

None truly happy here

Happy's that man, to whom God gives
A stock of Goods, whereby he lives
Neer to the wishes of his heart:
No man is blest through ev'ry part.

To his ever-loving God

Can I not come to Thee, my God, for these
So very-many-meeting hindrances,
That slack my pace; but yet not make me stay?
Who slowly goes, rids (in the end) his way.
Cleere Thou my paths, or shorten Thou my miles,
Remove the barrs, or lift me o're the stiles:
Since rough the way is, help me when I call,
And take me up; or els prevent the fall.
I kenn my home; and it affords some ease,
To see far off the smoaking Villages.
Fain would I rest; yet covet not to die,
For feare of future-biting penurie:
No, no, (my God) Thou know'st my wishes be
To leave this life, not loving it, but Thee.

Another

Thou bidst me come; I cannot come; for why,
Thou dwel'st aloft, and I want wings to flie.
To mount my Soule, she must have pineons given;
For, 'tis no easie way from Earth to Heaven.

To Death

Thou bidst me come away,
And I'le no longer stay,
Than for to shed some teares
For faults of former yeares;
And to repent some crimes,
Done in the present times:
And next, to take a bit
Of Bread, and Wine with it:
To d'on my robes of love,
Fit for the place above;
To gird my loynes about
With charity throughout,
And so to travaile hence
With feet of innocence:
These done, I'le onely crie
God mercy; and so die.

Welcome what comes

Whatever comes, let's be content withall:
Among Gods Blessings, there is no one small.

Eternitie

O Yeares! and Age! Farewell:
Behold I go,
Where I do know
Infinitie to dwell.

And these mine eyes shall see
        All times, how they
        Are lost i' th' Sea
Of vast Eternitie.

Where never Moone shall sway
        The Starres; but she,
        And Night, shall be
Drown'd in one endlesse Day.

To his Saviour, a Child; a Present, by a child

Go prettie child, and beare this Flower
Unto thy little Saviour;
And tell Him, by that Bud now blown,
He is the *Rose of Sharon* known:
When thou hast said so, stick it there
Upon his Bibb, or Stomacher:
And tell Him, (for good handsell too)
That thou has brought a Whistle new,
Made of a clean strait oaten reed,
To charme his cries, (at time of need:)
Tell Him, for Corall, thou hast none;
But if thou hadst, He sho'd have one;
But poore thou art, and knowne to be
Even as monilesse, as He.
Lastly, if thou canst win a kisse
From those mellifluous lips of his;
Then never take a second on,
To spoile the first impression.

Christs part

Christ, He requires still, wheresoere He comes,
To feed, or lodge, to have the best of Roomes:
Give Him the choice; grant Him the nobler part
Of all the House: the best of all's the Heart.

To his Conscience

Can I not sin, but thou wilt be
My private *Protonotarie*?
Can I not wooe thee to passe by
A short and sweet iniquity?
I'le cast a mist and cloud, upon
My delicate transgression,
So utter dark, as that no eye
Shall see the hug'd impietie:
Gifts blind the wise, and bribes do please,
And winde all other witnesses:
And wilt not thou, with gold, be ti'd
To lay thy pen and ink aside?
That in the mirk and tonguelesse night,
Wanton I may, and thou not write?
It will not be: And, therefore, now,
For times to come, I'le make this Vow,
From aberrations to live free;
So I'le not feare the Judge, or thee.

To his sweet Saviour

Night hath no wings, to him that cannot sleep;
And Time seems then, not for to flie, but creep;
Slowly her chariot drives, as if that she
Had broke her wheele, or crackt her axeltree.
Just so it is with me, who list'ning, pray
The winds, to blow the tedious night away;
That I might see the cheerfull peeping day.
Sick is my heart; O Saviour! do Thou please
To make my bed soft in my sicknesses:
Lighten my candle, so that I beneath
Sleep not for ever in the vaults of death:
Let me Thy voice betimes i' th morning heare;
Call, and I'le come; say Thou, the when, and where:
Draw me, but first, and after Thee I'le run,
And make no one stop, till my race be done

His Creed

I do believe, that die I must,
And be return'd from out my dust:
I do believe, that when I rise,
Christ I shall see, with these same eyes:
I do believe, that I must come,
With others, to the dreadfull Doome:
I do believe, the bad must goe
From thence, to everlasting woe:

I do believe, the good, and I,
Shall live with Him eternally:
I do believe, I shall inherit
Heaven, by Christs mercies, not my merit:
I do believe, the One in Three,
And Three in perfect Unitie:
Lastly, that JESUS is a Deed
Of Gift from God: *And heres my Creed.*

Another Grace for a Child

Here a little child I stand,
Heaving up my either hand;
Cold as Paddocks though they be,
Here I lift them up to Thee,
For a Benizon to fall
On our meat, and on us all. *Amen.*

The Bell-man

Along the dark, and silent night,
With my Lantern, and my Light,
And the tinkling of my Bell,
Thus I walk, and this I tell:
Death and dreadfulnesse call on,
To the gen'rall Session;
To whose dismall Barre, we there
All accompts must come to cleere:
Scores of sins w'ave made here many,
Wip't out few, (God knowes) if any.

Rise ye Debters then, and fall
To make paiment, while I call.
Ponder this, when I am gone;
By the clock 'tis almost *One*.

Tapers

Those Tapers, which we set upon the grave,
In fun'rall pomp, but this importance have;
That soules departed are not put out quite;
But, as they walk't here in their *vestures* white,
So live in Heaven, in everlasting light.

*   *

*

INDEX OF TITLES

H

INDEX TO FIRST LINES

213

*Two more recent additions
to the Penguin Poets are described
on the following pages*

SWINBURNE

Selected and introduced by Bonamy Dobrée

D55

It is now over fifty years since Swinburne died, and nearly a hundred years since his poetry flamed into the heads and bosoms of the poetry-reading public of the day. Young men in the 1860s would go about 'chanting to one another the new astonishing melodies' of the choruses in *Atalanta in Calydon*, or verses from the first *Poems and Ballads*.

No selection of Swinburne can be satisfactory to everybody, least of all, possibly, to him who selects. What Bonamy Dobrée has tried to do in this edition is to exemplify as far as may be every aspect of his poetry (avoiding for the most part the very long poems, though with regret); the passionate, the contemplative, the complex, and the simple contrasting those packed with ideas and the more easily assimilated narrative pieces, the vivid and the incantatory. The result is an excellent selection from the works of a poet whose surging rhythms and alliterative effects made so great an impression on the late Victorians.

BAUDELAIRE

Edited by Francis Scarfe

DATE DUE

A poet whose work is _____ and diverse, though
apparently so simple and unified, as Baudelaire's is not
to be summarized in any convenient formula. Yet
many attempts of this kind have been made; they are
useful and have to be taken seriously. A modern Dante?
This suggestion, first made in 1857 by Thierry, has
been discussed and modified by T. S. Eliot who would
be more satisfied with a comparison with Goethe. 'The
Swift of poetry', Lytton Strachey neatly suggested: but
they meet only in their disgust, wit, and gloom, and
Baudelaire is the bigger of the two. Aldous Huxley
called him 'a bored satanist' and Lionel Johnson stated:
'Baudelaire sings sermons'. He has been described as
'the tragic sophist', as 'Too Christian', and as a 'Near-
Jansenist'.

In this selection Francis Scarfe has placed the poems,
for the first time, in a roughly chronological order while
trying to preserve the 'cycles' into which they fall. A
plain prose translation is appended to each poem.